IRRATIONAL KINDNESS!

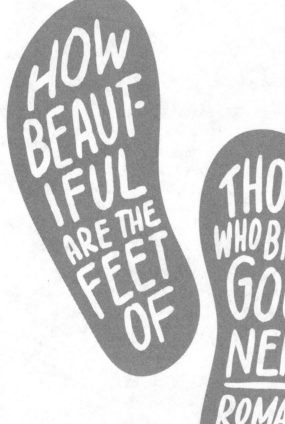

HOW BEAUTIFUL ARE THE FEET OF THOSE WHO BRING GOOD NEWS

ROMANS 10:15

IRRATIONAL KINDNESS!

The Crazy Pursuit of an Extraordinary Life

KEVIN WILLIAMS

NEW YORK

LONDON • NASHVILLE • MELBOURNE • VANCOUVER

IRRATIONAL KINDNESS!

The Crazy Pursuit of an Extraordinary Life

Published in New York, New York, by Morgan James Publishing. Morgan James is a trademark of Morgan James, LLC. www.MorganJamesPublishing.com

This book may be purchased in bulk for educational, business, organizational or promotional use. For more information, please visit irrationalkindness.com.

Scripture quotations are from the Holy Bible, New International Version. NIV. Copyright (c) 1973, 1978, 1984, 2011 by Biblica, Inc. Used by permission of Zondervan. All rights reserved worldwide. www.zondervan.com. The "NIV" and "New International Version" are trademarks registered in the United States Patent and Trademark Office by Biblica, Inc.

Chick-fil-A® and Icedream® are registered trademarks of CFA Properties, Inc. Used with permission. All Rights Reserved. The views and opinions expressed in this book are those of the author's and do not necessarily reflect the official policy or position of Chick-fil-A, Inc. or any of its affiliates.

100% of proceeds of this book go to support families in crisis and those with foster/adoptive children around the world.

ISBN 9781631952951 paperback
ISBN 9781631952968 eBook
Library of Congress Control Number: 2020943533

Cover Design, Interior Design & Illustrations by:
Meghan Brim
www.megbrim.com

Morgan James is a proud partner of Habitat for Humanity Peninsula and Greater Williamsburg. Partners in building since 2006.

Get involved today! Visit
MorganJamesPublishing.com/giving-back

BOOKMARK

Need a bookmark for your journey through the book?

We've got you covered.

Use the arrow to mark where you stopped reading.

 FOLD IT

 TEAR IT

 RIP IT

 CUT IT

 OR DON'T!

KINDNESS
PAUSE

As you read this book,
create time to reflect at
the end of every chapter.

You will see this icon
as each chapter comes
to a close, reminding
you to pause.

Feel free to use the space
on your bookmark to jot
down the chords you'll
use to write your
beautiful life song.

DEDICATION PAGE

This book is dedicated to Gwen, Mary Nell, Terry, Kate, Elizabeth and all the past and current Canton team members who helped me grow and who continue to teach me. I love being on your team.

TABLE OF CONTENTS

—

FOREWORD

BOB GOFF

Chief Balloon Inflator
Author of three NYT Bestsellers: Love Does, Everybody Always
and Dream Big

One of the challenges for soldiers in World War II was keeping their ammo dry. To address this, they would wrap the ammunition boxes in paper and then dip them in wax. This process kept the ammo dry to be sure, but when a soldier needed to get at it in a fight, they couldn't. Vesta Stoudt had two sons in the military, and she wanted her boys to get what they needed to fight the fights they were in. Vesta didn't just stay concerned; she got busy. After a lot of effort and even more creativity in the factory where she worked, Vesta showed her boss what she had invented. Almost predictably, her boss thought her invention was a lousy idea. Here's why: He simply didn't "get" what it was.

Sometimes people are the same when it comes to kindness, particularly the irrational variety. They just don't "get" what it is. There are several explanations for this. Fear, apprehension, and uncertainty would certainly top the list. Most people might think to themselves, a little kindness, sure, but why do a lot of it? Besides, who would it really help anyway? Everything in moderation, right? Why go overboard? The reason that kindness at this level is often hard to understand is that it hasn't been experienced. Simply put, it's hard for us to "get" what we haven't known.

Fortunately, Vesta didn't take "no" for an answer when her invention wasn't at first well-received, and we shouldn't either. She was determined to get the people she loved what they needed to fight the fights they were in. In a magnificent hail Mary, she sent her invention to then-President Roosevelt, who in turn sent what she had invented on to the Pentagon. Are you ready? This is how duct tape was invented. No kidding. It was an idea that was much needed yet completely misunderstood. In other words, some people didn't "get" it. Kindness is a lot the same. It's what can bind us together in our communities, our friendships, and our marriages. It what we need to fight the fights we're in, but sadly, it is often misunderstood.

We can always tell where duct tape is because it's shiny. We can also tell where it's been because it leaves behind sticky evidence. Here's why. Duct tape is meant to be effective, not beautiful. Gaffer tape, on the other hand, is what stagehands use on movie sets. It doesn't reflect light at all, and it comes off clean. There is literally no evidence it's even been there. Think about it this way: merely being polite with one another is gaffer tape. It has no shelf life. An irrational amount of kindness on the other hand, is duct tape. It's this brand of kindness Kevin talks about in this book, Irrational Kindness and kindness, like duct tape, is what we need right now to fight the fights we're in.

Kevin has been a friend of mine for years, and I've seen him live out the ideas he's written about in this book. This book isn't filled with impersonal lists of things to do or empty collections of words on pages. Irrational Kindness is a path I've seen Kevin walk in the workplace and his personal life. His hope for me and you is that we'll take the next courageous step in the direction of this over-the-top brand of kindness. If you will do this courageous work, will you be misunderstood by people who don't "get" it? Of course, you will. The reason is that you are you, and people are people. But here's the thing. The adventure is worth the effort to get there. So, buckle up and let's get started. You can forget having a bookmark. Just fold over a piece of duct tape. Here we go.

INTRODUCTION

The idea for this book—as with most of my good ideas—started over coffee early in the morning; medium-roasted Chick-fil-A coffee at 5:47 a.m., to be exact. It's been more than twenty-five years since we opened our first Chick-fil-A franchise restaurant in Canton, Georgia, and to this day, I invite all newly hired team members to *Coffee with Kevin*. What started as a casual conversation to welcome new employees to the Chick-fil-A team morphed into a more intentional welcome program that lets me sit down with them, ask about their dreams, and share my vision for our restaurants. It's become a cherished tradition that blends high-level discussions of company policies and expectations with personal truths and matters of the heart.

Along with having those more in-depth conversations, I began giving books written by some of my favorite authors to new team members during coffee time. Then one day it hit me: what if *I* wrote a book to give them? It could be full of stories about our fast-food journey at Chick-fil-A. It could include insights and inspiration, akin to those found in the books that I loved and had been handing out. It could recount all the things I never expected to learn—both in business and in life—from serving chicken. It could put many of the topics covered during *Coffee with Kevin* into book form. In that way, it could be a part-employee handbook, part-operating manual for how to thrive on earth.

Am I qualified to write such a thing? Not any more than anyone else. I proudly proclaim that I do not know everything, but I want to share what I do know. And it's with that intent that I wrote what you now hold in your hands.

While you'll soon see that each chapter stands on its own, there's an undercurrent that runs through them all. I want to talk about it here because I know how easy it is to miss a big plot sitting right in front of you. And well, because I love to kickstart a good conversation! Here goes.

Moving into my third decade of operating Chick-fil-A franchise restaurants, serving countless customers, and leading over three hundred employees—mostly Millennials and Generation Zers—I've learned one simple truth: If we want life to be an exhilarating adventure, if we want to find abundant joy, and if we want to accomplish great things on this journey, we need to get our brains around the concept of being *irrational.*

That's right. Irrational.

Often the idea of being irrational is smeared with negative connotations. It can sound illogical, senseless, unjustifiable, or groundless. It may even represent ludicrous and mad behavior! But I would like to argue that being irrational can be just the opposite. And it is the most positive, inspiring, and empowering way to be. Why? Because for our purposes, being irrational has to do with thinking outside the box—way outside. It has to do with viewing life as a journey and still being willing to reverse the route, shake things up, or flip the map upside down. Not just to *be* different, but to *make a difference.*

Am I irrational for writing this book? Some may think so. But if it helps you love your life, realize your value, and achieve your wildest dreams, then I'd say it will have been worth being called a little crazy.

In fact, there's someone I admire who was subject to a lot of name-calling back in the day. Maybe you know him? His name was Jesus Christ. He was about as irrational as they come, and his teachings make up the underpinnings of this book. Which teachings? Those of seeing the world and seeing ourselves in a different light—an *irrational* light. In Romans 12:2, the Bible reads, "Do not be conformed to the patterns of this world but be transformed by the renewing of your mind." Being irrational means constantly renewing your mind and remaining open to shifts in perspective.

Sometimes, just a quarter turn in perspective makes all the difference. Take failure for example. When we think in an irrational light, we can see negatives turn into positives. For example—

Failure becomes *opportunity*.

Frustration becomes *persistence*.

Deformity becomes *strength*.

Being last becomes *being first*.

Old age becomes *a second wind*.

Uncertainty becomes *a chance to dream*.

Problems and the things we can't control become an invitation to *start looking up to a big God who controls everything*.

This book is about how to live an irrational life. It's about living in a freestyle mode instead of following a scripted existence, and it's learning that just because something has always been done a certain way doesn't mean it's the right or only way. It's about finding abundant joy in our day-to-day journey, not just at the end of the rainbow, and throwing off the selfishness that so easily entangles us and living lives of kindness toward others—to give in life more than we take.

Jesus saw people and society, life and death, differently than we often do today. He was on a mission to care more about others than himself. To think irrationally, as he did, takes the weight of everyday life off us and transforms our energies and concerns into a spirit of service toward others. This, above all, is the spirit of kindness. And it's the most irrational when you make a daily choice to slow down to offer mercy, patience, and love to everyone. Do I mean our enemies and neighbors? Yep. What about foreigners and family? Uh-huh. How about the orphan and ourselves? Yes. Nailed it! So, all day, every day? Absolutely. And now, we are getting into some seriously joy-filled territory.

Think of this book as an operating manual for the heart—written for teens, moms, dads, students, retirees, recent graduates, and dreamers, all of whom are bound together by two empowering and sobering truths, which are that our jobs are much more than just jobs and our lives are about much more than serving ourselves. Allow this book to serve as a harmonious reminder that our hopes and dreams don't have to be derailed—not by our fears, our pasts, or by people who make us feel like we have to know everything to be successful, or even just to get started.

And with that, let's get started.

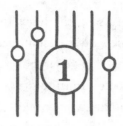

CHAPTER 1

CONSIDER YOUR CHORDS

---

*"All you need to write a country song is
three chords and the truth."*
- Harland Howard

I was ten years old when my parents said it was time for me to honor the family tradition of learning to play an instrument. I had narrowed my choices to either take up the guitar or sing in the Atlanta Boys Choir, which my parents allowed as an alternative to playing an instrument. My older sister had selected the flute and my brother the saxophone. One would think our family was a talented ensemble of musicians, but we all bordered on being tone-deaf and musically illiterate. It was *because* our harmonic gene pool was so shallow that the family requirement of playing an instrument was designed —it also encouraged us to stretch our brains' learning capacity.

After much internal debate, I chose the guitar. Years later, my

friend John Mellencamp sang the lyrics that expressed the senti-
ments that had informed my decision exactly: "You may find a
cushy job and I hope that you go far, but if you really want to taste
some cool success you better learn to play the guitar."

My parents and I unknowingly selected a guitar teacher who
turned out to be an amazing guitar player but an awful instructor. In each session, I'd strum along to songs he would play loudly
over the stereo. I remember trying to catch on to Lynyrd Skynyrd's
"What's Your Name" and Steve Miller Band's "Fly Like an Eagle."
Some of the chords I played didn't sound like they even matched
the songs, but my instructor rarely corrected me, and the music
was so loud it drowned me out anyway. I never learned to pick
strings or do barre chords. We just stuck to the simple up-and-
down of strumming.

Since I was hungry for some cool success, I continued taking lessons from this guy anyway. I began to strum the handful of chords I
knew amazingly well as if it were as easy as reading a children's book.
As I attempted to expand my musical playlist, my limited ability
forced me to stick with songs that only included my inventory of
kid-friendly strumming and chords C, E, G, F, and D.

My favorite thing to do became writing my own songs because
when I attempted popular songs like Simon and Garfunkel's
"Bridge Over Troubled Waters" it sounded totally troubled. I
felt overwhelmed and incompetent when I was asked to copy
someone else's killer guitar riffs or solos. So, I found that I could
use my simple strumming style, playing only a few chords, to
pour out my heart in melodic poetry. Soon, songs about my dog,
my room, and my friends began to emerge from a playground of
endless creativity. In my mind, I was speaking to the world when
writing songs that cried out for justice, adventure, and peace. My
Generation X anthem "Check Your Gauge" proclaimed

Win or Lose, Yes or No, it's cut and dry to me
11-0 or 0-10, either president or a hobo
They put a monkey suit on you at an early age
You sing and dance with the rain
Play your cards right middleman and check your gauge

The point is that by learning guitar I learned an irrational truth—that when it came to music, just a handful of chords could take me anywhere I needed to go, and I could create anything I wanted. With that freedom, I recorded an album of songs. Now, mind you, I did it in one session in a guy's basement studio, which I found in the classified section of the newspaper. But I did it. And although I'm nothing more than an elementary-strumming, five-chords-only guitar-player, I wrote and recorded an entire album.

I am thankful for that scary yet rewarding experience because it taught me that I only need to know a few small things to accomplish great big things. None of us needs to know every chord to write a beautiful song, just as we don't need to know every "chord" to build a beautiful life. In life, these chords are the foundational behaviors, beliefs, gifts, and talents we can choose to offer to the world. If we can identify the key chords we want to play in our own lives, then we can enjoy the freedom to create the life of which we dream.

I've listed some of my favorite life chords, which I'm sure you'll recognize:

Kindness	*Hopefulness*	*Gratefulness*
Curiosity	*Courage*	*Creativity*
Peace	*Patience*	*Persistence*
Joy	*Rest*	*Fun*
Failure	*Freedom*	*Honesty*

While I've leaned into some of these more than others through-out the years, they are the fundamental tenets that I strive for and construct my life around. I truly believe that holding tight to these basic chords is how I've managed to have any personal or professional success. They certainly paved the way for me to join Chick-fil-A and have kept me going strong as a franchisee over twenty-five years later.

As a bootstrapping entrepreneur, Chick-fil-A Founder Truett Cathy followed his own set of chords. In 1967, exactly two weeks after I was born, he designed a franchise model that would allow someone like me, who had very little assets, to own his or her own business. By providing a single restaurant franchise with very little upfront cost, he sought to partner with people who would be passionate and persistent business owners. In 1991, I pursued this opportunity with Chick-fil-A for three reasons: an absence of cash, a love of business, and a chance to lead a team with a purpose. I figured I'd be able to make a difference in the lives of team members and the community while enjoying the thrill and challenge of competing in business.

After a two-year pursuit of Chick-fil-A, I was selected in 1993 as a franchisee for the Colony Square location in downtown Atlanta. The existing restaurant had been open for several years, but it was losing money every month. Giving me an unprofitable store was a safe bet for Chick-fil-A. How bad can he mess it up? was probably the talk around the water cooler during the selection process.

The following years at Colony Square were far from easy because, let's face it, not earning a profit is fun for only so long. Since I'd spent more than four years prior working in banking, I knew very little about the ins and outs of running a fast-food restaurant. But I did know that, as in any industry, employees who don't feel engaged or valued are unlikely to care about the details of the business. The restaurant business, in particular, is relentlessly transactional. It quickly became apparent to me that we would have to intentionally redirect our attention toward the internal relationship side of the business *every* day because, more than anything else, caring for our team members would have a profound impact on the cost of other things, such as food, labor, and paper—not to mention nearly every other expense!

In those early days, I worked as hard as I ever had to start building relationships with every team member. I saw that building these relationships would be the driving force behind managing quality and cost. I also believed this investment in people would make the biggest difference in moving the needle toward a more desirable bottom line, financially and relationally. It took an irrational commitment of time and energy, because, unlike a high-cost line item on a profit-and-loss statement, relationships do not always scream "*URGENT!*" I went against the current of conventional business practices by first spending time on the important work of building team-member relationships instead of focusing on the urgency of number-driven transactions and results. This people-centered strategy proved to be the rock a team's foundation could build on—and I love a house built on rock.

Slowly but surely, our team began to care for guests and each other in new ways that made the work much more exciting and meaningful. Instead of asking team members to take orders, it became more like asking them to dance—in that back-and-forth, ebb-and-flow, two-way-street kind of way. Our new paradigm opened the door for conversation where once there was only a script. It created a team bound by clear accountability toward one another, where before there had only been a lack of long-term commitment. It fostered an environment of trust, where before there had only been uncertainty. After about six months, we became profitable for the first time. That first dollar we made in profit made me feel like I had reached the summit of Mount Kilimanjaro.

Reflecting on my professional journey, I can see that my life chords have underscored my entire experience. They've guided my outlook, actions, and growth as a business owner, team player, and boss. Did I know anything about owning or operating a drive-thru? No. That's where *curiosity* came in. Did I second-guess my decisions and feel like I was out of my depth? All day. *Courage came in.* Did I do everything right? Heck no. *Failure.* Did I call on others for support and guidance? Humbly so. *Gratefulness.* Did I encourage myself and my teammates to keep hustling even when it seemed like we'd never make it out of the red? You bet I did. *Persistence.* Did I lead by example teaching the importance of servanthood, regardless of conventional reasoning and business policy? I always tried. *Kindness.*

I try not to play favorites, but kindness has arguably become the most important chord we play at Chick-fil-A Canton. We go so far as to tout "Kindness Over Everything," and internally refer to the chord as "irrational kindness" since it goes far beyond holding doors open or being friendly to strangers. To us, irrational kindness is much more active. It means that regardless of the situation, our actions will exude generosity, grace, mercy, and service above every other emotion or action we may want to exhibit. It reminds us to stay kind, respectful, and courteous even when we hear something we don't agree with or understand, and the courage to stay, even when we don't see progress. It's important to note that this level of kindness does not mean selling out, giving in, or getting run over—it simply means being kind, even when it seems *irrational.* That entire concept challenges us to operate from a different perspective and see through a different lens in both work and life.

Consider the chords you're going to use and begin putting them into practice as you write the beautiful song of your life. You may be sixteen, forty-five, or eighty-six. Age doesn't matter. I urge you to take your passions and your God-given talents and pursue your dreams. Shoot for seemingly unreachable destinations using only a few simple life chords. You don't have to know exactly how the song you're writing will turn out on the final album of your life, but the secret to success is to start by building whatever you can with your key chords and personal truths. Declare the chords that are important to you and start strumming them loudly. It's a more exciting, irrational way of giving and experiencing life; one that breaks through the conventional wall of reasoning that limits us and our dreams.

We have another saying at our restaurants in Canton: "If you think you *can't*, you *can* in *Canton!*" It's a spark, an expression to remind our team, our community, and ourselves that if we set our minds to it, we can do *anything*. I love to hear the words "we can," especially when sung as a chorus. It is an unstoppable chant.

Together we can be curious and explore ideas to help us succeed in navigating business, family, relationships, and the world. Let's continue writing the amazing songs of our lives using only our handful of powerful chords. Sound irrational? Think you *can't?* Repeat after me: "I *can* in (your hometown)."

‖

KINDNESS PAUSE

What is one chord you'd want to start strumming today?
What distracts you from practicing that today?

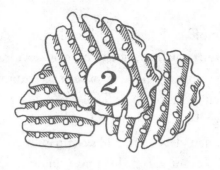

CHAPTER 2

WAFFLE FRY COOK

―――――

"You can't complain about the results you didn't get from the hard work you didn't do."
- Coach Mike Krzyzewski

"My dream is to flip burgers," said no one, ever.

"You're going to end up cooking fries the rest of your life," might be a line that someone like your teacher uses to illustrate the lowest position you can hold among social hierarchies. And if your daughter wants to marry a french fry cook, you may even have a few choice words of advice for her on that decision.

But hold on a second, folks. My name is Kevin, and *I'm* a french fry cook. Since we cut our potatoes into uniquely crisscrossed waffle patterns at Chick-fil-A, I'm technically a *waffle fry* cook!

I've never enjoyed a view from a fancy corporate office window where I sat in an executive chair in a corporate meeting and discussed how to create a new corporate paradigm for organic growth.

Neither was my office designed with mahogany and exotic linens and perfumed with fine fragrances. I have no doctorate in the study of organizational management or experience running cross-functional departments that produce fiscal-year budgets for a large corporation. I don't lead psychological research studies or calculate statistics in human development, sustainability, and growth. In fact, I am 100 percent sure I don't even know what those things really mean.

I often marvel at the beautifully written, seemingly magical words I read in leadership books authored by men and women who have actually led very little. That, however, is not this story. Instead, most of my experience has been as a *grinder*—someone who gets up before five each morning to turn on the kitchen ovens in preparation for the first batch of biscuits. I believe it's by the diligent work of tireless grinders that cities get built. It's we who pave the roads, construct the buildings, lay the plumbing, feed the workers, and paint the town. Our alarms go off early and we stay as late as it takes to get the job done. I've worked with thousands of people, young and old, in a fast-paced, ever-changing environment that revolves around preparing chicken sandwiches 311 days a year (we're closed on Sundays). I've worked in urban restaurants in the heart of downtown Atlanta and in suburban restaurants at the edge of the mountains in northern Georgia. *My* ivory tower is a fluorescent-lit room covered in biscuit dough, seasoned coater, and peanut oil. My problems are not solved in a higher-education research lab, but in the back of a cramped kitchen where delivery drivers are constantly knocking at the door to bring supplies into our restaurant. Our boardroom is made up of a small table in the back of our restaurant's dining room, which is often busy and noisy.

Sometimes I sit in the crusty seat with the broken arm and crooked base that we keep in the restaurant office. The chair sits on a tile floor that needs to be cleaned frequently, near yesterday's cash tills that are $86.34 short and the broken Icedream machine that the night crew mended with a straw. Sometimes I have felt stuck in an environment where sales were stagnant and profitability was in jeopardy; where we needed to find new people to hire because Cindy the biscuit maker called at 5:30 a.m. to tell me her dog was too sick for her to come in, and Tom just quit because he decided he was overstressed at work.

And guess who doesn't care? The customers who are walking through the door. They don't want to hear about the problems I have to handle in the office. All they want to hear us say is "My pleasure!" with a smile and a perfectly prepared four-pack of Chick-n-Minis. Oh, and they want to know if we can make it quick because, by the way, they're in a hurry!

The point is this: life is hard! That's a fact, Jack, and I get it. Even when our Chick-fil-A restaurants are bustling with customers, our team members are taking care of all kinds of problems behind the scenes. And, on the surface, you may not see how hard it is, but what I hope you can see is a waffle fry cook who is simply trying to get a little better every day.

You see, I grew up with buckets of doubt, fear, and insecurity about not measuring up in a world that looked like it was all put together. I was a nerd who often didn't know how to fit in, who had a history of stumbles and falls. I know both the fear of being bullied and the ignorance of bullying others. I have stereotyped and been stereotyped. In your mind, you may have already put me in a box. It's easy to do that to each other. Yet even though life is hard, jobs are tough, relationships are tricky, and people let us down, none of these things has to define us.

If you're reading this to small children, be warned: I am about to use the S-word. Ready? Here it comes… If you feel like things *stink* where you are, then high-five a friend or someone next to you because you are on a launching pad, ready to take off. That *stinking* is not going to own our *thinking*. It's going to provide us with an opportunity to shift our mindset to find excitement in life's seemingly constant uphill pedaling, especially when we realize it's going to be such fun coasting down the other side of the hill. In other words, the stink is a sign that your surroundings or situation may require you to make a change for the better. However, the key is to learn to be positive through your transitions and uphill pedaling. Although, it's easier said than done.

Being positive requires that we reset the mind by getting down to the heart of the matter every day. You can reset by allowing more time, more grace, and more consideration in the way you approach your challenges. So much of life is made up of routine things like managing schedules, school, job hunting, working, dating, and parenting—just to name a few! All these things are normal, and you can't untangle normal. But you can begin to live out your purpose just by giving yourself a break. My friend Don Henley sings "The Heart of the Matter," which is all about forgiveness and the need for a little tenderness, but forgiveness and tenderness start with showing a little *kindness* to yourself. And remember, Rome wasn't built in a day, why would you be? According to Google, it took 1,000 years to build Rome. Remember that when you need to give yourself some grace. (You can Google *grace* too if you need to.)

Often, what I'm doing in the fast-food industry is simply learning how to get better at managing the tough parts of the business. The reason any of us are hired in the first place is to help solve problems. We all become more valuable to a company and its customers by responding intelligently in the trenches. So rather than always looking for a way out of a difficult job, we can improve much more by digging for fresh perspectives in our work.

We all recognize that a flashlight illuminates much more in darkness than in light, so think about how and where your light is shining. I would suggest that if your life is all about your own personal advancement, it makes it very difficult to shine like a flashlight in the dark. Your light may only be lighting up your own feet. And your boots may look pretty, but you can't see where you're going.

When you redirect your heart *outward* toward those you can serve, you're suddenly on the way to lighting up a very bright path. This approach means the waffle fry cook is doing more than just putting fries in cartons. He or she is fueling the next generation, nurturing conversations between moms and daughters, brightening peoples' days by being a positive influence in the kitchen, and using a potato to create a community that supports each other during good times and bad.

I have seen this play out at Chick-fil-A through a corporate purpose that was written by some of the company leaders at a retreat in the early 1980s. At the time, Chick-fil-A was located only in shopping malls, and it was burdened with a mountain of problems: floundering sales, debt, and economic issues. So, its leaders took a figurative and literal step back to explore new strategies that would help move them forward. Amid fear, anxiety, and stress, the leadership decided to give themselves some grace, and they used it to ask themselves who they wanted to be during this season of pain. Most of the time, it's not easy to give yourself this kind of space and margin because you're eager to solve the problem immediately. But they essentially asked themselves, "What is our definition of success?" Stopping in the middle of their turmoil to think about their heart and purpose was an unexpected, if not irrational, approach because it tied their joy into something greater than the inevitable ebbs and flows of the business. The Chick-fil-A corporate purpose they wrote then still stands today: "To glorify God by being a faithful steward of all that is entrusted to us and to have a positive influence on all who come into contact with Chick-fil-A."

The first part of their statement acknowledges their desire "to glorify God" during *both* the difficult and the rewarding times that occur working in fast food. They were reminding themselves that they didn't want their work to be all about themselves. Then they added the phrase "being a faithful steward of all that is entrusted to us." To me, that means we don't actually own anything, but rather we are custodians of this life. This both takes some pressure off and puts it back on. Isn't that peculiar? Think about it. When I own something, it is mine. I wrap my arms around it and guard it close to use as only I choose. Yet, when I see myself as a steward of something, that changes how I keep it in my heart. Now, I extend my arms to hold it out with open hands to be blessed by God and used according to his plan. The idea of *wanting to leave it better than it was when we arrived* challenges us at Chick-fil-A to live out stewardship as a service to others. It allows a fast-food worker, or anyone, to see his or her work and problems in a new, brighter, and clearer light.

This way of being is what makes me proud to say I work at Chick-fil-A as a waffle fry cook. I know my purpose is not just selling a chicken sandwich, but building community with customers, vendors, team members, applicants, recruits, the town of Canton, and the world. It is not about seeing others merely as transactions, but as people with whom you want to develop relationships. It's about creating moments of kindness. And the best part is you can apply this irrational approach to any profession and to any of life's challenges.

Going through challenging seasons can be difficult, but we're all going to go through such trials. It may be because of the bad decisions we made or perhaps it's just the cards life has dealt us. It could be because of family drama, bad relationships, laziness, or anxiety. Heck, it could be because you're simply getting older and have more responsibilities than when you were a child. Work is hard! Don't blame me. Blame Adam and Eve. Trust me, I would have done things totally differently—and probably would have messed it up royally. Still, one thing I have experienced firsthand is that we can learn and grow and improve right in the middle of all our challenges. Make up your mind to speak positively, even during life's trials. Carve out space in your brain to see things differently, to think a little irrationally. This kind of thinking can hit you like a breath of fresh air, with all the tingle of a Tic-Tac. It's a modern-day mystifier. But don't get derailed waiting on everyone to get on board with your thinking. Grab a pen and write down your own purpose statement about how you want to live your life. At the end of the day, it's your life. In fact, at the beginning of the day, it's your life too.

Take Jozsef, for example. He's a team member at our Chick-fil-A Hickory Flat restaurant. He is a kindness freak and Satan's worst nightmare. A customer recently wrote me a note about him that read—

One of the employees (Jozsef) is there every time I go, and EVERY time I've encountered him, he has had the biggest smile and the most positive attitude I have (possibly) ever encountered...even at 6 a.m.! My kids even comment on how genuinely happy and kind he is every single time we see him! This morning, I finally asked him, "How do you keep such a positive attitude all the time?" He thought it over briefly before responding with, "I'd say it's a combination of perspective, being a people person, and just overall knowing that God's got my back."

Jozsef is on a journey to be intentional with his perspective. He incorporates a love for people in every interaction. He is not just a money taker but an experience maker. I love being on Jozsef's team and learning about how he deposits kindness in the bank of relationships. Sure, he could spend his time and emotion differently, but he makes the decision to take another road—He sees a bigger vision for his life. On that road, he carries a belief that we can do more with generosity, kindness, and purpose than we can with the quick, cheap responses we are often pulled toward. While serving sleepy guests in a fast food restaurant at 6 a.m., Jozsef decided his love for others would help write his purpose statement. Armed with the values of love and persistence, he is single-handedly flipping the kingdom upside down.

Of course, my greatest example is Jesus, who was known locally as a carpenter for much of his life. He was in the blue-collar industry of building and fixing things with his calloused hands. He did that for most of his life, and you can imagine much of his work was difficult and challenging. So why isn't he best known for his construction skills? Because alongside his work, he lived out a purpose; sometimes recommending things that were irrational. Like the belief that when someone forces you to go one mile, you should go with them two miles. He shared how he was not defined by religion but as a servant of kindness for outsiders, undesirables, sinners, and even waffle fry cooks. Hey, that's me!

Our kindness muscles will be developed by creating moments of kindness; moments that do not always feel urgent but are extremely important. What if we gave ourselves a break by not assuming all our assumptions are true? What if we took a page from the Master Playbook and discovered these moments of opportunity in the face of the hidden inequities, discriminations, and biases of the world? This means being merciful toward people who are totally different from us—getting a cup of coffee with them, carrying a tray to their table, picking up trash in the parking lot of a competitor without telling anyone, or turning a job into an opportunity to love our neighbor. Jesus's purpose was a message of love for others that we not only get to still hear about over two thousand years later but also get to try to emulate.

Let him remind you that if you find yourself in the middle of a tough job, down in the trenches, you are in a *perfect* spot to live your purpose. Darkness is often where we learn to see. Weirdly, when there is no light, we begin to see ourselves clearer. So, seek out and grow into the things you love. Optimize your brain to create in these areas. That is where growth happens best and where purpose can be made clear. Everyone has different passions, formal education goals, hobbies, and activities they enjoy, but pushing yourself to grow in the things you love is something we can all do. It's the difference-maker! That's the kind of thinking that allows a fast-food restaurant in Canton, Georgia to be a spotlight into the world. That is my journey in the trenches, flipping chicken and cooking waffle fries—just the kind of job your teacher warned you about.

KINDNESS PAUSE

In your daily routine, what brings you the most joy?
What would you have to give up to spend more
time doing that?

CHAPTER 3

SIXTY-FOUR

*"Ships are safe in their harbors but that's not
what they are made for."*
- Gwen Williams

He was sixty-four. I was a teenager. The year was 1985. Truett Cathy, the founder of Chick-fil-A, was coming to Tucker, Georgia to talk about his life as an entrepreneur. *Entrepreneur.* That's a mighty fine word, and I am here to tell you it frustrates me. It is hands down the most difficult word in the English language. No one knows how to spell it and eight out of ten humans can't pronounce it. Google defines it as a person who organizes and operates a business or businesses, taking on greater-than-normal financial risk to do so.

I would quickly learn that this entrepreneur I would get to hear speak that fall day was defined by much more than simply operating a business or taking on financial risk. Truett Cathy was more like a gunslinger in the business world, kicking down doors and taking names. His nametag read Truett Cathy, but it could have read BA of the CFA. He ate risk for breakfast, failure for lunch, compassion for dinner, and drank a milkshake for dessert. He played outside of his own sandbox. An intimidating menace to corporate America, he was like a Beastie Boy that rolled into town on a Harley Davidson. He didn't need to know how to spell or pronounce *entrepreneur* because he had Chuck Norris do it for him.

I was a teenager inspired by a man who had spent sixty-four years shooting out conventionality with a vengeance. You see, at the time, I had been busy building my own personal conglomerate for a few years. When I was twelve, I took over my brother's grass-cutting business when he went to work for Ace Hardware. I mowed about three to four lawns per week and dreamed of owning a slew of lawnmowers and trucks that would expand my empire. I was motivated to work because my parents had made it clear there would be no bow on a surprise car waiting for me when I turned Sweet Sixteen. My father had earned his first car by picking prickly cotton in the hot Georgia fields, and I was going to earn mine by mowing neat rows of grass in the suburban Georgia fields.

I feel fortunate to have been raised in a home where my parents modeled how a commitment to working hard, showing love, and living within your means could produce long-term results. My dad worked at Ford Motor Company, and my mom was a nurse-turned-real estate agent. They did not encourage me to go on a journey of self-discovery to find my innermost being by traveling the world. Rather they told me to go to work and let my hopes and dreams evolve while working hard at my job. Though it's considered old-fashioned, it's beautiful advice for which I remain grateful to this day. It helped me understand that dreams could be built on the solid foundation of hard work and honesty.

My landscaping corporation never expanded out of the Summertown neighborhood, but it did create an entrepreneurial spark in me that fueled a desire to have my own business. I didn't know it at the time, but that spark would land me in a front-row seat where I could watch Truett Cathy's life unfold for the next thirty-five years.

That day in Tucker, Truett shared how he was just eight years old when he started purchasing six-packs of Coca-Cola for twenty-five cents, loading the bottles into his red wagon, and turning around to sell single sodas for five cents each. Every six-pack he sold earned him a five-cent profit and this margin ignited Truett's love for business. In the middle of the depression, his mother ran a boarding house and his father had little involvement in Truett's life. Truett would cook for the boarding house guests and sell copies of the Atlanta Journal-Constitution newspaper to help make ends meet. As a challenged student who struggled with grades, he decided to join the Army after high school and subsequently served in World War II.

Following his service, Truett managed to scrape enough money together to open a tiny 24-hour diner in Hapeville, Georgia, where he served guests six days a week, in 1946. He called it the Dwarf Grill and went into business with his brother, Ben. Two years later, Ben tragically died in a plane crash along with their other brother, Horace.

For the next twenty years, illness, fires, and failed business decisions all contributed to the adversity that fueled and narrowed Truett's focus. Instead of giving up, he leveraged the space he found himself in to create a chicken sandwich. Drawing on his cooking experience, he began hand-breading a choice cut of boneless chicken, cooking it quickly in peanut-oil pressure fryers, and putting it on a toasted, buttered bun with two crucial pickles.

In his mid-forties, he was brave enough to introduce the idea of selling food in shopping malls. It wasn't an easy task, as he often had to face down mall developers who didn't understand his commitment to being closed on Sundays. He spoke their language, though, and slowly but surely proved to them Chick-fil-A could generate more revenue per-square-foot than their other tenants.

Truett's life was not just defined by a chicken sandwich, but rather the way he used *the influence of the chicken sandwich* to invest in the next generation. He talked passionately about the importance of others, of both attracting and keeping hard-working young people, and making them a priority. This influence extended to providing loving homes for children in foster care, building summer camps for boys and girls, and investing millions of dollars in scholarships for employees.

Truett was radical in his belief that a great business was all about people. This way of thinking started with his untraditional, unique, and potentially crazy business model. By providing an opportunity to own a restaurant with little upfront cost, he found a way to foster the dreams of young men and women. His generosity toward people touched every corner of his business, as he offered free daily lunches for all Chick-fil-A corporate employees, annual trips for franchisees and their spouses, and Lincoln Continental giveaways for high performers. Above all, Truett shared the unique view that his relationships with his franchisees were like a marriage—one that always protects, trusts, hopes, and perseveres.

He was often stealthy in sharing his mountain-high kindness and the way he followed his unrelenting view of serving every guest the right way. On the day he spoke in Tucker, he said a lot about simply being your best and valuing a good name over great riches.

I soaked it all in. Truett was different. A disrupter in the marketplace, and completely dangerous to the competition. I mean, he was building a business on a foundation of the courageous, relentless belief that nothing was more important than caring for others; he focused on building a good name and long-term relationships over positional power or financial wealth. Now *that* is playing dirty.

What began with me listening to a speech from the founder of Chick-fil-A in 1985 eventually led to me becoming a three-time Chick-fil-A franchisee decades later. There is one thing I learned from Truett that continues to impact me today. When, in my mind, I wasn't making the progress I'd hoped to in life, this truth cleared a path for me to continue working toward my dreams. Get ready for it, because this truth is still just as profound today as it was then. Ready?

Truett was sixty-four.

Yes. So, when you're getting down on yourself or there's negativity all around because you haven't reached certain goals and dreams in life, think of Truett and keep working! It could just mean that you need to revamp your strategy and break out of the malls (literally and figuratively)!

Yep, that's it. That simple bit of information is something I've reflected on and used to my benefit hundreds of times in my life. You see, I had expected cool success by the time I was twenty-five years old—and that was me being patient. But here was a story I could remind myself of countless times: Truett was in his mid-sixties when he shared his life story that day in Tucker. The Chick-fil-A we know now was really just getting started back then, and the only Chick-fil-A locations open at the time were in malls. It would take seventy-three years for a six-pack of Coke to become a multi-billion-dollar organization.

This realization forged a new direction for me, not just in work but also in life. It became my encouragement in the face of failure, when I dreamt too small, or when my dreams seemed unattainable.

It was one critical point that has helped me reboot my thinking many times since then.

I was selected as a Chick-fil-A franchisee when Truett was in his mid-seventies. In his eighties, he was starting a new "My Pleasure" initiative and building new relationships that would serve business leaders and ministries around the world. In his nineties, Truett was leading the creative endeavor for a new restaurant concept called Truett's Luau. The principle he taught me, that I've had to remind myself of numerous times, is just how easy it is to miss the story of the long expedition and only see folks as they are now.

It's human nature to see a huge success in something or someone and to simply gloss over all the challenges and trials the person experienced up to that point. If I weren't careful, I would have missed the history of the young Truett Cathy who spent his first twenty years grinding hard in Hapeville, Georgia, where he worked eighteen hours a day, six days a week, running his diner—long before he ever launched his first Chick-fil-A.

I would have bypassed Truett in his mid-forties when he took a chance on his first Chick-fil-A restaurant at Greenbrier Mall in Atlanta. I would have missed his unflinching commitment to the principle of putting people first by refusing to open his restaurants on Sundays—despite pressure from his competitors and mall developers. Here was Truett, standing in front of me at the age of sixty-four, with all the energy of a man in his twenties, advising us not to wait until we "made it" to have significance. He shared that it doesn't matter what you do *for* work, but rather what you do *with* your work that matters.

I love what Truett said to me one day when visiting his office after I'd become a franchisee: "Remember how important your job is. The responsibility we have to treat the customer right every time is huge. If an employee mistreats a customer or serves poor quality food, then you could lose that customer for a lifetime. People forget the price they pay for a sandwich, but they do not forget how you made them feel."

People come to our restaurants to have their coffee cup and stomach filled, but they also want their hearts filled by smiles and respect. I could argue the same is true for our team members. They come to have their bank accounts filled and their hearts. Why not always do both? It costs zero dollars to the bottom line to have a joyful spirit and go the extra mile to brighten someone's world. Truett is proof that excellence starts with being *better*—to others and ourselves—every day. He exemplified that success is fleeting, but excellence endures.

Life is not a quick elevator ride to the top. Instead, it's full of unexpected stops that allow us time to take inventory of how we act, who we are, how we treat others, and how we treat ourselves. Give yourself the grace and space you need to ride the elevator all the way up and grow into who you're meant to become. Social media would have us believe that we must own a house, have sixty thousand followers, and travel regularly to new countries all by the time we're thirty, making life a sprint rather than a journey worth savoring. I'm here to tell you that your value as a person is not determined by any of those things. Studying the life of Truett Cathy from beginning to end has given me much-needed truth, clarity, and perspective on the self-imposed pressures we are subject to live under today and has helped me to clear my own path to a fulfilling life.

I often visualize myself on a trek through a jungle swinging a machete to clear my path. The brush is thick, but I know there is an oasis up ahead somewhere. I'm with a guide who is swinging away on his own path nearby. It's Truett Cathy. He's alongside me on the journey in my mind, and I make a point to keep one eye on him.

I don't want to go right along on the same trail he's on, because that one is his and not mine. But I want to always know where he is so I can see clearly that I'm headed in the right direction. I can clear my own path with my machete, but it helps to listen for my guide and follow him along the way as he reveals new wisdom and possibilities on his path to that oasis.

Other times, I visualize myself on a stroll through Walt Disney World. Have you ever noticed that when you ask for directions to a specific ride at one of their parks that they always point with two fingers? Try it for yourself some time. Ask an employee how to get to It's A Small World and watch them direct you with the two-finger approach instead of one pointer. This move strikes me as a kinder, gentler way to direct patrons when compared to the harsher, one-finger approach. The idea here is to find someone or some organization you trust to help point you kindly in the direction you want to go. Choose not to follow someone who directs you in a one-finger-pointing-know-it-all kind of way, but someone who offers you a two-finger approach that will help you grow and give you the caring, compassionate direction you need. As I seek wisdom, courage, and direction in the dense forest and tangled vegetation of life, I've found it helpful to find people who can help me visualize the path I need to clear for myself.

We all have the advantage of looking down the road and seeing how the story unfolded for Truett Cathy. In my twenties, when I felt rushed to have it all figured out, the testimony that Truett Cathy had not even opened his diner yet allowed me to give myself some grace. In my thirties, when I experienced challenges that felt like dead ends, I could see Truett dressed as Mickey Mouse. He pointed toward my path with two fingers, reminding me he was still running a tiny diner at that age. In my forties, when I thought I should be accomplishing more and having a greater impact, my jungle guide reminded me he had not even broken ground on Chick-fil-A yet. Now in my fifties, I can look back and see a Truett with only a handful of mall locations, wondering if his business would be a success.

If you're sixty-four and wondering if you missed the mark, well, chill out, Mr. Bojangles! Because the Truett I heard speak that day in Tucker was sixty-four, and he was just beginning to break the surface on the impact he would have on this earth. Which guide you're following matters much more than your age. Listen to the guide who asks if you're getting better every day. Listen to the guide who reminds me, as Truett reminds me, "Yesterday is history, tomorrow is unknown, the present is God's gift to us to do with as we choose." Those words are here to point you and me in the right direction—with two fingers, of course.

And if you're twenty-four and you have RSF—the official abbreviation for Resting Sad Face—tattooed on your sleeve because you haven't struck gold yet, then rest assured knowing that you, too, can be cured by looking toward a guide who has nerves of steel. Be irrationally kind to yourself and trust that the joy is in the journey. Find someone who focuses on building lasting excellence rather than temporary success. For me, that someone was the two-finger-pointing, machete-wielding, Clint Eastwood of the chicken sandwich empire. For you, it will be someone who teaches by example that patience and persistence are required to grow and embrace your own journey every day.

If you have trouble finding a guide, Jesus's life is one you can study and rely upon. It gives you a window into the world of an explorer who went before you to point you in the right direction; to provide a path for you to see, admire, and walk alongside. Jesus gives me and you *space* to be me and you. He gives us the freedom to forge an enduring path in a life that is not a sprint. He switched gears in his thirties to leave carpentry and gather some friends to start a movement. That movement proved to be an act of irrational kindness, which demonstrated that the way we treat each other matters, and it often begins during a meal with a stranger. Or over a cup of coffee and a conversation with someone who is different from us.

Whether you like it or not, I know this about you: today is a day for you to pour yourself into relationships and to go against the grain. It's a day to leave your worries and cares behind because you can trust that there is a guide walking with you. When we lift up the pursuit of excellence ahead of the fleeting dream of success, then we can clear a good path with our proverbial machetes.

I realize you may try to rock the casbah and you may hit rock bottom. Crap happens. People let you down. Companies fail. A pandemic arrives. You're not guaranteed success just because you follow someone awesome. Emulating a great company does not automatically mean you'll create a billion-dollar business. Being patient and persistent doesn't mean you'll win every race in life. But hear me out: When the importance of claiming a victory evolves into the importance of developing endurance, the whole game changes! If you stop trying to rush through each of life's adventures with the speed of Usain Bolt, you can begin marching confidently to the beat of excellence and the cadence of kindness every day. Time and age become less significant factors. Being your best each day becomes the biggest win.

Let's face it: We are all gathered here today to get through this thing called life, as Prince reminded us. Walking through that life with a great teacher can make your dreams come alive. Try to enjoy the simple act of forging your path alongside your guide. Give yourself some space to learn the lessons he or she is teaching. A little misstep only requires a little course correction. Never be so focused on the destination that you miss the journey—or the guide that's cheering you on. Breathe in a breath of fresh air and see today as your chance to be a little better than you were yesterday. Heck, in your search for the right path-clearing guide, you may discover a faithful sixty-four-year-old travel companion, as I did, or maybe a wise thirty-year-old carpenter to lead you through time and across the globe. Both are irrational entrepreneurs, one who slung kindness with a chicken sandwich and the other with a cross—each one a flare through the darkness for all to see.

KINDNESS PAUSE

Which living person do you most admire?
Why?

CHAPTER 4

PEOPLE'S CHICKEN

*"Success consists of going from failure to failure
without loss of enthusiasm."*
- **Winston Churchill**

I don't know about you, but I love things that are deep-fried and simplified. No one got this idea of simplicity better than a chicken restaurant near the University of Georgia that felt like it was custom-built for college students. I was just beginning my college journey in Athens, Georgia when I first stepped foot inside Guthrie's on Baxter Street. I fell in love, true love. The menu was made up of chicken fingers, fries, Texas toast, coleslaw, and a secret sauce that pulled it all together. Just five things! I had never seen a place with such an intentionally small menu that was flooded with so many customers. The chicken tenders were prepared fresh and the secret sauce was good enough to drink. College students with big smiles and bubbly personalities would take your order with a genuine spirit of youthfulness. Over the next few years, Guthrie's and I furthered our relationship by spending huge amounts of time together.

After steadily pursuing Guthrie's for years, I decided it was time to take our relationship to the next level. I wanted to become an owner. Guthrie's only had a few locations, so I took a wild guess at the names of the owners and looked up Mr. and Mrs. Guthrie. I got a hold of their phone number and made the call. When Mr. Guthrie answered, I nervously asked him about becoming a franchisee. I didn't bother telling him small details, like the fact that I had zero money in my bank account, or that I was barely old enough to be considered an adult. Instead, I explained how I dreamed of owning a Guthrie's and joining the fight to conquer the world one chicken strip at a time.

He shot me down in a blaze of glory. He explained that he had explored the idea of franchising in the past, but he had no plans to allow anyone else to take part in owning another Guthrie's. I watched my dream of serving chicken as it taxied down the runway. And then I decided it was time to start my own restaurant.

I was working in banking and lived with friends in a home we called the Heron House, a name we took from a song by an Athens, Georgia band we loved, R.E.M. We asked everyone who visited the house to take a picture standing alongside a poster of R.E.M.'s lead singer, Michael Stipe, and then we posted it on a wall for all to see. In a house where there was a revolving door of activity, it made old and new friends feel welcome.

Inspired by this open-door spirit of hospitality, the Heron House became the birthplace of our soon-to-be restaurant chain, People's Chicken. My roommates and I partnered with a noble vision: chicken for everyone—all people, everywhere. It was going to be all about the guests for us; a place where everyone felt welcomed. That meant *everything* to us. It was going to be a place that thrived on community impact, with a heart for global causes. "Think Globally, Eat Locally," would be our slogan. The way we saw it, People's Chicken was going to change the world.

We knew that one of the biggest keys to establishing our global movement would be cracking the code on the secret sauce. We spent countless hours perfecting it and holding tasting parties to get it just right. Then we needed suppliers. We needed a place to get the chicken, the oil, the fries—all of it. Under the cover of night, we decided to dumpster dive behind Guthrie's. Parking on a side street by the restaurant and silently approaching the dumpster, we thought of ourselves like Navy Seal Team #6. It was well after closing time and everyone had gone home. In the dark of night, we scavenged that dumpster like miners. Every used label, fry bag, and mayo packet we found was like striking gold. We put everything we thought we could use as evidence and loaded our cars for the two-hour trip back home.

Once there, we inspected each piece of trash in great detail like we were on an episode of *CSI*. We learned what brands they used, what size products they purchased, and what manufacturers they bought from to prepare their chicken in all its saucy goodness. Armed with all this intel, People's Chicken now had the tools to begin setting up a supply chain. With a restaurant name, a marketing slogan, a global vision, and the magic sauce in hand, we knew we were gaining steam.

The next few months were a whirlwind. We met with landlords and negotiated deals. One landlord offered us a space we could have rent-free for the first few months, contingent only upon signing a lease. It was here that People's Chicken came to a crossroads. Taking this step was going to mean each of us would have to take on a significant amount of investment and debt. That was the prerequisite for being *entrepreneurs*. Staring down the point of no return, I had to stop and ask myself, "Am I actually going to do this? Is this a wise decision?"

I hate to let you down, but I must tell you…this was where the People's Chicken dream died. It's sad, but it's true. At the time, I was embarrassed to admit that we shelved the dream when it came time to write the check. But we all knew, deep down, that none of us was really ready to take the leap, sign the lease, and quit our jobs. The risk was just too big for a few college buddies back then.

The worst part was that I'd spent so much time telling people about the dream and the ending seemed completely anticlimactic. But here's the thing: while I could look at the People's Chicken story and easily label it a failure, that's not how I choose to see it. I'll be the first to admit it can be a total bummer to see a journey like that come to an end after investing such a great deal of time, energy, and emotion into it. Feelings like jealousy, doubt, and embarrassment may creep in unexpectedly. That's okay. You can sit with those feelings and give them grace too. Just don't stay long enough to build a house there. Moving forward in the face of feelings like these shows true bravery—and it requires nothing more than taking the first step. We all have the opportunity to see disappointing circumstances and daunting challenges in one of two ways: We can see the situation as the bigger the obstacle the bigger the chance of *failure*, or we can see it as the bigger the obstacle the bigger the chance for *discovery*. I chose the latter. Of course, I was sad the restaurant was not going to become a reality, but I never regretted pushing the idea to its brink. I could still say that I went for something and learned a ton along the way. The only wasted time is the time you spend *not* pursuing an idea you're passionate about.

People's Chicken taught me some practical things about business. One thing I learned is that franchises and restaurants are expensive to build—especially when your funds are so low that your rap name, if you had one, would be Lil' Money. The second thing I learned is that dumpster diving is messy and doesn't teach you everything you need to know about supply chain management. And the third thing I learned? Forming partnerships is weird because it presents its own challenge of bringing together different personalities to make an even greater plethora of things work.

People's Chicken taught me some amazing life principles too. The journey of having an "unrealistic" idea and still going after it is a journey of self-discovery all on its own. Failing at that pursuit accelerates learning. And pushing forward, even when failure is likely, can be a brave decision to make. If an appropriate risk exists and a noble purpose follows, then you stand to gain more by taking that first shuffle than not. Dance the first step of your dream. Don't let those who sit on the sidelines and toss pebbles of doubt or hate dictate every move you make, every breath you take. Whenever you choose to mix and mingle with life's bold endeavors, there will almost surely be failure, ridicule, and folks trying to bring you down. Instead of letting them, learn to turn the page by celebrating your failures!

That's right, I said it. If you've ever failed, you should be *celebrating*. Throw a party. Build a *wall* of failures. I've done just that at my house, where I set up a wall that proudly displays my mountain of failures for me to see plainly. Here are just a few on my list:

After playing soccer my whole childhood, I got cut at tryouts during my senior year of high school. I have no jersey to frame, but I do have a framed picture of the Parkview High School soccer team *without me* in it.

A stock certificate valued at $25,000 also hangs on my wall of failures. Having poured the majority of my savings into this new bank start-up, the stock dropped to $0 when the bank went bankrupt. A hot tip gone bad; another lesson learned.

There is a picture of me in front of hundreds of people at the opening of our second Chick-fil-A location, and in it, I have the sweatiest armpits you've ever seen. Not one person told me about the awkward stains. I walked around that day as proud as a peacock in my blue dress shirt, clueless, like a dog wearing the cone of shame.

I have four counterfeit tickets to the Miami Dolphins vs. New England Patriots game, for which I paid more than $1,000. Not to mention the fact that I'd bought the tickets after reading (and making fun of!) an article about how to avoid getting suckered into buying fake tickets. Oops!

Then there's the Big Hit. One day my football coach called the kickers of the team, which included me, over and suggested we were wimps. We needed to toughen up, he said, so he was putting us in a tackling drill. On the first drill he put me in, I got nailed so hard, head-on, that both my contacts popped out of my eyes. My teammates unsuccessfully scoured the dirt searching for my contacts. Since I have atrocious vision, I had to be escorted off the hot field and to the payphone—a long walk of shame—where I could call my mom's beeper so she could bring my glasses, and I could drive home. Ugh.

We all have stories like these that remind us of what seems like an embarrassing failure. My wall is designed not to remind me of my mess-ups, but to help me remember that I am alive and kicking! Each "failure" that hangs on my wall represents a yellow brick in my road to growth and success. I suggest you make your own list and hang it on the wall. Not so you can wallow in remorse or constantly be reminded of all your failures, but so you can look back at how you conquered every fear and overcame every obstacle. Calling out these past experiences helps us understand that they don't have power over us and exposes the lie our brains tell us that we are no good. Focusing on this lie can cause us to lower our heads for so long that we miss the next opportunity. Remember, recognizing your missteps is not about going around apologizing to everyone about your failures; it's simply about praying each day for the wisdom, courage, and knowledge to better understand your journey in its entirety.

Exposing failure reminds me that I'm still here— breathing— right now. Now, the first step: breathing. Now, if you're not breathing, this exercise is unnecessary. And if you *are* breathing right now, then let that be a reminder that life goes on. We are not defined by our mess-ups and failures. We *will be* defined, however, by our failure to *try*.

If you ever feel stuck in your failures, consider the story in the Bible about a guy named Paul. He was massively mean, rude, and naughty. He persecuted and relentlessly ridiculed people with whom he didn't agree. Fast forward a few years, and you'll find Paul using his past experience to propel him toward a place of love for all mankind.

Although I never had an episode like Paul, who was blinded and underwent a name change, I do have my own set of failures that have molded and shaped me into the person I am today. We can all let our failed attempts lead us to a place of courage and kindness. Paul is defined now by his commitment to faith, hope, and his greatest encouragement, love. I imagine Paul underwent a ton of hiccups as he transitioned from a life of hate to one of love. From him, we can see that failure isn't always a sign from God that you need to stop moving altogether. Rather, it can be a sign of God coming alongside you to help you find clarity in taking your next steps.

Going after your dreams is just a matter of putting on the right shoes for a little baby dance. One baby step leads to the next baby step. And as we discover new things about ourselves and others, another stride is revealed. Cue Miley Cyrus singing in the background as I tell you that you can't climb the mountain in one step. She reminds us: "Sometimes I'm gonna have to lose. Ain't about how fast I get there...It's the climb." People's Chicken didn't require me to jump off a cliff. It simply urged me to climb by taking one little, fearless step after another.

So often we build up the steps in front of us into something so big and daunting in our minds, it can lead us to inaction. You may find yourself thinking things like—

"That step is too big. I might fail."
"I've always had that problem. I have no control over it."
"I can't actually make a difference."
"I am so far behind everyone else."
"I'm just not good enough."

Maybe you've heard someone else say these things before or maybe you've said them to yourself. What do I have to say to that? "That's true, that's true." A saying that my team and I inherited from Patrick Baker—a longtime CFA employee—and we now use as a response when someone points out the potential failure or the difficulty of a task. "That's true, that's true," we say in a fast, funny voice that always brings out a smile. There is something honest and positive about acknowledging that we might not always know how to get from point A to point B. What I do know is this: it will be a learning experience no matter what. In fact, thriving often comes at the end or even in the middle of crying.

My first chicken-restaurant journey took a route I could have never predicted. It went from a business idea to a dumpster dive to a lease left unsigned. But, as it turns out, celebrating failure can pave a new path for a brave discoverer. Think about it. What are your dreams? Write them down. Pick one and tell folks about it. Want to be in a sitcom? Go ahead and share that. Want to eat dinner at the White House? Share it. Want to be a high school teacher? Share it. I have found people love to help others achieve their dreams. Embrace your spirit of curiosity, and then see who rises to meet you.

Oh, and those failures on your wall? Let those be your secret sauce. See them as a mix of all the different ingredients you've tried in life, each one getting you closer to the perfect recipe. Join God in looking at them as reminders of the awesome adventures you've had, the amazing things you've learned, and the inspiration for the direction of your next steps.

KINDNESS PAUSE

What is a crazy dream you have that you'd like to pursue?
If that dream were a movie title, what would it be?

CHAPTER 5

JAVA BEACH

"Just let go of control, trust in me.
Let me be, your cornerstone. Be still."
- Christina Semeria

Snowflake was the name my family and I gave to the white fifteen-passenger van we rented when we headed out on the adventure of a lifetime in California. There were thirteen of us who boarded Snowflake in Los Angeles for a summer road trip that would take us up the California coast and then eastward for a grand finale in Las Vegas. Unlike her namesake, Snowflake was hardy. She carried us through all types of weather, from rainstorms and snowfall to 110-degree heat. Together we were ready to discover all the greatest wonders of the West. We visited enormous celebrity homes in Beverly Hills, towering waterfalls in Yosemite, and the vastness of the Grand Canyon. What I didn't expect was that none of these would be the highlight for me. Instead, I fell in love with a coffee shop—one that would shine as a beacon of light for the rest of my life.

When we got to San Francisco, we spent days soaking up all the smells and swells of the bustling city nestled against the Pacific Ocean and basking in the shadows and the beauty of the Golden Gate Bridge. Our first day, we decided to get started by gathering everyone at a coffee shop near our hotel. The Java Beach Cafe was a little slice of heaven that came alive the instant you walked in and caught a whiff of the overwhelming aroma of freshly roasted coffee. The employees took special care with the fresh fruit and pastries they served. They played relaxing music and people constantly came and went, kick-starting their days so happily it was intoxicating.

For our group, it instantly became a place of restoration and rejuvenation. It was a place where we could connect, reflect, and plan; where we gathered around cups and cups of conversation at the start of our days. We found Java Beach to be an oasis where we found restoration during our great adventure. In fact, it meant so much to us that "Java Beach" became our family nickname for any place that gives us space for restoration and reflection.

Now, I realize that restoration is not always our greatest priority in the modern world. We're constantly connected to mobile phones, social media, 24-hour news cycles, and extended workdays. Yet, it is during this chaos that we need space most. It is here that restoration whispers to us, "Stop. Be quiet. Savor the margin of white space." This space is where we're called to reflect, where we are called to be still, where we can allow our hearts to soar and be thankful. Here we have no hidden agenda and we can simply appreciate every breath of fresh air we take in.

I have learned to find spaces like Java Beach in all types of places throughout my life. It can be early in the quietness of the morning.

It can be found as far away as the lobby of the Glenlo Abbey Hotel in Ireland or as close as a corner you pray in at the foot of your bed. It can be found lying on your back at night under a starry sky or rolling into bed early and lying still under the comfort of an eye mask. Maybe you find it sitting with a group of coworkers as you talk about life over lunch. Maybe it's in calling up a friend you respect, sitting down with them, and discussing your life's journeys. Your Java Beach can be any place of restoration that substitutes the agenda and busyness for quietness and space. Milli Vanilli blamed it on the rain, but I blame it on our hurried souls. We don't give ourselves the restorative space we so desperately need.

I have become both a student and a fan of this idea of restoration, of giving yourself a margin. Margin is the avenue that provides time and space for a human being to seek rejuvenation and repair the soul. As a matter of fact, our business at Chick-fil-A is built upon these principles. Chick-fil-A creates a substantial margin for its employees and its guests simply by being *closed* on Sundays. That's the beauty of being irrational. Think about it. You'd have to be out of your mind to forgo sales on the busiest fast-food dining day of the week, wouldn't you? It appears nutso! Yet Truett Cathy called it the best business decision he ever made. Today, operating just six days a week, Chick-fil-A averages a significantly greater number of unit sales than its nearest competitor. To know that our team members, guests, and equipment are all getting some rest and relaxation is a powerful concept. It seems worth exploring how this space and rest can actually be the reservoir fuel that propels us further in life.

Despite its appeal, it won't be easy. In fact, you will need the bravery of a lion and the diligence of a beaver to pursue quietness in the tumble of our ever-busier, hyper-connected world. You will need the strength of the greatest warrior to fight for the space to reflect. And restful Sundays won't always equal easy Mondays. Just taking a day off work won't solve every problem. True restoration takes time and work that almost never ends. However, living at a constant warp speed simply means you're being unkind to yourself. And why would you be unkind to that person, of all people? A little bit of light changes a whole lotta darkness.

In Genesis, the story of creation gives us a good example of this principle. God himself gave a margin for restoration during the flurry of the week's activities. There is no doubt that creating the entire universe, including night and day, people and animals, was a big project to tackle. But, as the tale goes, on the seventh day the Creator set time aside to rest, to be blessed, and to honor that time as holy. It's irrational, isn't it, that to get *more* done we need to do *less* at times? But I can promise you that it will be worth it for every one of us to find margin where we can investigate our lives.

Quite frankly, it will require every ounce of courage to explore the principle of margin and put it to the test. To discover this place of restoration and reflection, you'll have to stand up to the bully of busyness and allure of money. It can seem impossible when there is so much to do and so much that we want to accomplish in life. Often, we believe we should fill every available moment trying to check off those tasks. But remember that there's value in creating space for much more than binge-watching TV, wandering the mall, or playing video games. This personal-Java-Beach idea I'm talking about is something else. It has to do with doing *less* of something that, in turn, becomes doing something *much more*.

While it may be difficult, powering down and removing hurry from your heart will allow your brain to investigate spaces you've never explored. So many amazing things can be revealed in this quiet space! That can be scary at first. You might not know what to do with your hands in this open space of time if you are lucky enough to find it. Looking internally and examining what you're doing or where you're going demands bravery. To confront and embrace this need for reflection is to give it a home every single day. This is the way to shine light on decisions, direction, gifts, and imperfections.

Benjamin Franklin accomplished amazing things for mankind during his time on Earth. He helped found the United States of America, moved us forward by harnessing electricity and furthered our education by starting a university, among other things. But he did so by taking the time to contemplate his movements rather than rush through his days. He intentionally started each day by asking himself, "What good shall I do this day?" Then he ended each day by asking the question again, "What good have I done this day?" This single moment allowed him to reflect upon and organize all the things that made up his life—both in his mind and on paper. Committing to this daily discipline gave Ben Franklin time to reduce hurry and distraction, which helped him determine who he wanted to be and what he wanted to accomplish in life.

This concept of intentionality may sound simple, but it is not easy to accomplish. You can grow your courage by scheduling monthly "thinking days" in a coffee shop, a public library, or anywhere quietness is encouraged and cell phone usage is not. Then, if you want to really test your bravery, step up to an annual two-day personal planning retreat and give yourself space to identify next steps for investing your time toward family, work, and community. Building time for quietness to explore the person you are and the path you're on allows God to speak into that space.

In fact, daily devotions are one practice of margin and restoration that has worked powerfully in my life. For me, it includes time spent in prayer and time spent journaling while reading verses in the Gospels, the Epistles, the Psalms, or the book of Proverbs—

and it always provides a great kickstart to my day. Do what works for you during this meditative time and have fun thinking crazy. Ask yourself unexpected questions, like what if you were to become a police officer? What if you were to learn about acting? What if you painted a picture? What if you ran for county commissioner? What if you became a parent to a child in foster care? What if you planned to hike a new trail? What if you got intentional about becoming friends with someone of another ethnicity? What if you wrote a book about the thing that matters most to you?

As you learn to give yourself margin, try to extend that courtesy to others as well. They, too, need the gift of space to grow. Some of the best team members at Chick-fil-A turned out to be folks who did not start out as rock stars. While asteroids that light up the sky are an unbelievable sight, they tend to burn up quickly, but when you invest in creating and encouraging a margin for others who need space to discover their greatest strengths, that can provide a gift of astronomical proportions.

See for yourself! Invite someone out for coffee, tea, or a smoothie. It can be someone you work with, someone at a different level in your organization, school, or community. It's as easy as finding the phone number, email, door, or desk of a person who's different from you. Then calling, emailing, knocking, or walking over to them and asking to learn more about their life. It's about showing up and being more interested in learning about them rather than dominating the conversation to share about yourself.

See how taking some Java-Beach time can bust up some serious divides between yourself and others! Learn to be an advocate and ally for your brothers and sisters of all backgrounds by kneeling with them in quietness. Transform individual preferences, beliefs, and hopes into collective care for each other.

Giving this type of space to a person of another generation, race, political party, sexual orientation, country, or religion may feel weird at first. Sometimes it was downright uncomfortable for me when I began intentionally putting this into practice in my life. In fact, sitting in the margin is often *about* awkwardness; you may feel uneasy about the silence, you may learn surprising things, you may not know what to say. But the only way to kill the power awkwardness has over you is to embrace it. That's when you get to reap the rewards that come from simply listening to, learning from, and empathizing with the person you're connecting with.

Develop a sense of curiosity toward others. Ask more questions than you give answers. Since you're not in their shoes, ask questions about their shoes. Find out where they came from and where they're going. You'll discover some amazing things—about them and yourself.

You should know that creating margin for yourself means you may disappoint someone. It means accepting that you can't be everything to everyone all the time. It means you may have to stop doing certain things to create more space for thinking. You'll likely have to give up something to create margin in your life because there's no option to add more hours in the day. That means the obvious solution is to simply quit something. Quit reading some news. Quit excessive TV time. Quit notifications. Quit bad relationships. Quit snoozing your alarm. Quit staying up late. Quit it already. This journey of creating margin to find your Java Beach will have tradeoffs that are not easy.

For instance, it was disappointing for my father-in-law, Simon Dixon, when we stopped serving coleslaw at Chick-fil-A several years ago. It was his signature move to put that coleslaw on his Chick-fil-A sandwich. To him, we weren't just removing this product after seventy years of serving it; we were killing his cherished sandwich-slaw concoction. Yet, we needed to make room for new options that catered to the next generation of diners. Building margin is not always about stopping something bad but often about creating space for growth; and time has proven that the risk we took was worth it in the end.

Keeping in mind the challenges, think about what you will need to give up to create a margin of space that has the potential to unlock some real depth and clarity in your life. Go, discover your own Java Beach. Reserve time for a nap. Go for a walk. Have a breakthrough. Make a list. Slowly say the word "tranquility" to yourself five times at night. Forget your phone for a day. Try to think differently when you find yourself on autopilot. Take a picture that represents restoration and let it sing to your soul. Soak up a location where you have room to roam in quietness and open the door to a space of fearless self-reflection that God can speak into. Breathe in through your nose and exhale through your mouth the oxygen of God as you...pause.

Give God the space to expose the opportunities and give yourself time to uncover the steps that can propel you forward. Use this time to move intentionally toward your goals, hopes, and dreams. See the progress that takes place in these margins. Set out on a quest to find the beauty in the margin represented by your own Java Beach. If you choose to add this margin, this wiggle room, to your life, it may well be something you look back on in amazement. You may surprise yourself and declare it the best decision of your life—even among all the other wonders.

KINDNESS PAUSE

What's your Java Beach?
Where do you experience your Java Beach?

CHAPTER 6

LOOK UP!

"When I'm not feeling my best I ask myself, 'What are you gonna do about it?' I use the negativity to fuel the transformation into a better me."
- Beyoncé

I'll let you in on a little secret: I love the Indigo Girls. This folk-rock duo has been singing to my heart since the first time I heard them strum their acoustic guitars. In my opinion, Amy and Emily combine to create the perfect mix of thoughtful and melodic music, with a blend of simplicity and complication, that completely captures the heart. If you've ever heard the song "Kid Fear," you know what I mean. The third song on their first major album begs you to re-evaluate the things you're afraid of, and I lose it every time collaborator Michael Stipe, of the band R.E.M., sings the question, "Are you on fire?" It ignites a sense of passion, beauty, and agony over a world of possibilities. I see it as a challenge, in poetry form, to put aside the childish ways of dealing with life and reboot my approach.

One night, they were playing a surprise, one-of-a-kind show in a small music venue. It was the buzz of the town, but I hadn't been able to score a ticket to the sold-out show. My friends and I went to the venue hoping we could still get in. As huge crowds gathered outside, it became clear everyone was scouring the area for tickets, just like we were. With no tickets in sight, our feelings of hopefulness quickly escalated into feelings of desperation. Fortunately, there is something about staring down a roadblock that can spark creativity.

Stepping back to assess our options, we noticed a van had pulled up at a side service entrance to deliver items for the show. And *that* became the sign for our detour. We piled back into the car and drove to the nearest convenience store on the hunt for the biggest bags of ice we could find. Each of us took as many bags as we could carry. Back at the venue, we walked up to the service entrance where the van had stopped and entered casually with our bags of ice—completely undetected! We delivered them to the concession area, placed them behind the counter, and calmly walked to the center of the concert hall, where we promptly erupted into high fives. Our plan was in no way elaborate or foolproof, but it wound up being just crazy enough to work—and our persistence proved to be worth it. Our coup was followed by what is now recognized globally as one of the best performances in history—at least in my world. There was even a surprise guest appearance by Michael Stipe, who belted his amazing part in "Kid Fear." I kid you not.

I have learned in life that obstacles often arrive out of nowhere. We can be strolling along life's day-to-day adventures, excited about the numerous possibilities and opportunities ahead of us, but then suddenly run into a dead end. It feels like walking into a turnstile that won't turn; instead of pushing through, we just bump into it. So, we back up, curse our luck, and try again. We ram the turnstile even harder, only to have it reject us a second time. We instantly feel embarrassed, ridiculous, and frustrated. We blame the stupid machine, the manufacturing company that made it, or anyone we can. Life will be full of locked, malfunctioning, annoying turnstiles—it's guaranteed.

The vexations that have the power to derail us can come from many places—politicians, news outlets, coworkers, bullies, outcomes, misinformation—all of which can drive us crazy. They can be so real, destructive, and insensitive that you respond by narrowing your focus on the problem or the person in your mind until it's all you see. You stare down at the broken turnstile in frustration as you repeatedly throw yourself against the barrier that will not open.

What can we do when we run into them? We can illegally leap over it and risk getting arrested. We can bang into it over and over, only to be repeatedly rejected, or we can back up and look up. That's right. *Look up!* Just as we did outside the Indigo Girls show, when we saw the van and devised a new path inside. If we had kept our heads down looking for tickets, we would have never seen the open door right in front of us.

This played out for me early one evening when I was stuck in an irritated state of mind. I went for a walk with my black, ten-pound poodle, A.J., and explained to him how I was feeling angry about the way someone in my life was behaving. They had refused to do something I wanted them to do, and I had spent days overanalyzing every possible scenario of the situation. I'd been getting more and more frustrated about this situation and people who were not acting the way I wanted them to—both of which were literally out of my control.

About halfway into my walk with A.J., I did something unusual and difficult to do in these types of situations. On this particular day, I *looked up*. You know what I saw? A big, beautiful sky that seemed to stretch as far as the eye could see. I saw clarity in my smallness against the magnitude of the universe. I embraced the vulnerability of how dependent I was on the air I breathe, and I felt gratitude for the earth that provided this air. And the thing I saw most clearly was that this magic had been right there the whole time. I was so fixed on problems that were out of my hands for the first thirty minutes of my exercise that I completely missed the miracle of the huge sky above me. I could imagine the depth beyond how far I could see and realized that I was just a speck in the galaxy. The world I was seeing was one grain of sand on the beach. The solution to my problem was not in the handful of options my small mind could come up with. Heck, it may not have even been for me to solve. My eyes filled with tears at the realization of the magic all around me. I was overcome with emotion because seeing the sky instantly reminded me of the one thing I do have control over: the power to look up.

Trust me when I say you have the same power. We tend to believe that the longer we stare at the problem, the more likely we are to solve it. But staring is not polite. Do you like it when people just stare at you? No? Then quit staring at things you can't control. Instead, stare upward and see what other avenue opens up. It's extremely easy to do, physically. Just grab your chin and push it up. Then draw your eyes up to the sky, pausing ever so slightly to explore the horizon. I like to take a deep breath through my nose and then exhale through my mouth slowly. Try it now. I'll wait.

When you look up, you can see a horizon that goes far beyond your current problem. You can see that this is just another of life's challenges that you need to grind through. You can discover new routes that were hidden from view when you were staring at your problem. You can see a God who loves you in a really big world. You can feel small (in a good way) and see that it can't all fall on your shoulders. You can uncover gratitude you hadn't noticed but had been there the whole time.

There is so much to discover by simply looking up. You may find other people, more time, new directions, or the voice of God to help you sort through your problem; the discovery of looking up is going to be a big problem for your problem.

One of the best things we can discover by looking up is people who can help us. It's true. If you look long and hard enough you will see others come alongside you. Sometimes they are difficult to see because of the plank stuck in our own eye—a plank of anger, jealousy, prejudice, disappointment, or selfishness that can blur our vision. But helpful people are all around if you know where to look. You don't have to look for an army of folks to solve any one problem, just one person can make all the difference. He or she may be found in your community, local business, church group, or service organization. They can live right under your nose or just outside your comfort zone.

Looking up may also reveal people who are destructive. You may see clearly that just because someone says something about you or your situation doesn't mean it's true; it just means they said it. It may mean they are mean-spirited. And when you look up, you can see that they are not God, but rather just regular people who are as flawed as you and I. In looking up, you can see that the high road doesn't require you to respond arrogantly, with a parting shot of hatred. Instead, you can lay your sword down and look up to discover the kind-spirited people you want to include in your life.

You may also find that looking up often reveals the fact that people simply have different views and opinions than you do. You can see that you are not in charge of how everyone feels, acts, or sees the world. I don't know about you, but I can get really caught up in feeling like I have to weigh in on *everything* for *everyone*. That's when I remind myself that kindness is in our availability to listen and not in the answers we give. Really, you are only in charge of your own views and behaviors. It takes courage to seek out fresh insights from other people, especially people who may tell us we are wrong. And when we receive these insights, it also takes courage to show irrational kindness to ourselves and others instead of beating ourselves up over what went wrong or staying in a relationship with someone we can't change.

The real reward is looking up across the horizon to seek people who need a friend and seeing that *you* may just be that person. You may make the fresh discovery of a group that needs your help. Looking up takes our view off our problems and finds opportunities to serve others instead. Looking up makes it so you can see those blessings! It takes constant effort to move our perspective from hate to love and when we stare at our problems, we miss our opening. Redirecting our energy to see the needs of others above our own is the best turnstile ticket I've ever found.

The gift of time is another discovery you can make while looking up toward the sky. Exploring and expanding the horizon of your time gives your troubles a shot in the gut. Problems and people who give you problems despise it when you give yourself the gift of time. Conflict and adversity are made more difficult when you feel you obligated respond in a split second. But what if you have twenty-four hours? What you *need* to say in that email or text will become much clearer if you wait. Some wise counsel once told me that nearly every response needs twenty-four hours of breathing room. If you don't take time to look up, you may feel you need to force a hasty answer or response—and you may say something you wind up regretting. When you allow yourself time to take a deep breath, you may find you need a day, week, year (or even more!) to get it right. Like Rod Stewart sang, "Young hearts be free tonight. Time is on your side." Slow down your cadence, take a deep breath, look up, and give it time.

Looking further down the line of time allows you to see that your struggle may be just the thing you need to move forward in the new direction God has planned for you. Maybe you didn't get what you wanted at the end of the day. The fact is you can't control what you can't control—like the weather! But we know from every airplane ever flown, there are blue skies above the clouds—100 percent of the time. They are up there, somewhere. Your answer is up there, somewhere. So, just keep looking up for new discoveries in direction, attitude, and options. It may require you to find a new flight path or a higher altitude, but that's not a problem. You now have the key: Look up because your attitude determines your altitude.

Opening one of our Chick-fil-A locations required our developer to remove a nearly seventy-year-old building from the property. Even though the building had been left vacant and dilapidated for fifteen years, it had served as a country store for many years before that. It was filled with wonderful memories of our city's past and that meant it was emotional for our community to lose it in that way. Some in the community started a petition to save the building, and social media in our town began to buzz around the loss.

In all honesty, the building was unsalvageable whether our restaurant went there or not; the county had already determined that its footprint was too close to a road expansion planned for the near future. We could have easily gotten mad at the people voicing their opinions and pushed back. We could have been upset with the direction our new adventure was taking. Looking up made it easier for me to hear the voice of Carly, an eighteen-year-old team member, who shed light on another path: "Kevin," she said, "we didn't tear down a community landmark, we're *building* a community landmark. Kindness over everything!" Getting her head above the storm clouds of the situation, she was able to see further down the road. Her perspective shifted our story from one of negativity and discouragement to one of opportunity and progress. She reminded us all that we were getting a chance to create new memories in our city over conversations, Coca-Cola, and Chick-fil-A chicken.

When we find ourselves at an intersection of struggle and inadequacy, God can become more alive to us and clearer in his direction and wisdom when we look up toward heaven. Looking up reminds me that it's not all about me. We can be reminded of just how small we are and just how big God is. Quite frankly, my dear, it takes the pressure off. In exploring the creation of that big sky, the stars in the universe, even the design of the ground we walk on, we can feel how amazing God is. We can hear his Spirit in the sky cheering us on, reminding us to "be strong and courageous" because he is everywhere on the journey with us. We can begin to see the outcome of a situation is often not dependent on us, but a Higher Power. Giving the problem a margin invites God to enter and gives him space to work his magic. Rest in that thought for a while. You don't have the power to conquer everything, but you do have the power to allow God to do so. Be kind to yourself by giving him space.

Explore the kindness this life offers by seeking the grace God gives. We're all incredibly free to go down this road and recount the things we have. It shocks the system into the pursuit of discovery. It helps me to simply pray with gratitude for the simple things in life. I am breathing. I have a dog. I have a heart. I have a number one with a lemonade—or at least I know where to get one. Give thanks for what you have easily and place all that is difficult in the hands of the one who created this world. Give grace and get grace.

Many years after my Indigo Girls ice caper, I was waiting on a flight home from Memphis. I was sitting quietly on the floor by myself, away from the crowds at the airport terminal, when a few people sat down next to me. When I finally looked up, I saw that those people were Amy and Emily of the Indigo Girls. In what felt like the most remote part of the airport, my heroes had come to sit side-by-side with me on the heavily trafficked floor. With my heart racing, I turned to Amy and confessed my devious behavior from the ice caper, which illegally gained me and my pals' entrance to their show years earlier. Thankfully, she loved the story! And I saw it as evidence that when you look up, you sometimes find incredible surprises you never expected.

The ability to look up wreaks havoc on those "Kid Fears" Amy, Emily, and Michael sang about in that concert years ago. It stands in complete contrast to our immature ways of staring at adversity with anger, fear, and sorrow. Looking up shows us that we don't have to continue with our infantile ways, but can, instead, recruit a little patience and curiosity. Looking up is a kick in the pants to your kid fears.

When you have problems that feel insurmountable, grab your chin and move it up to the sky. Remember that you are a navigator of options. You may not know why the things you can't control are standing in your way or where they stand exactly, but you also don't know where they are leading you. They might just be signposts for your next adventure. Fear doesn't stand a chance when we quit staring at the jammed turnstile and start looking for the horizon of faith, hope, and love; when we look up to unveil a beautiful blue sky of possibilities, full of time, people, direction, and God. How irrational!

KINDNESS PAUSE

Look at the sky. For sixty seconds, breathe in through your nose and out through our mouth. What fresh directions or resources do you see?

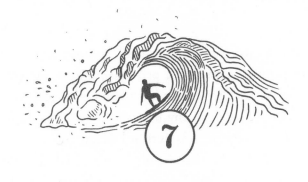

CHAPTER 7

FREESTYLING

"We don't follow the rules, we set standards."
- Ally Love

My son Terry and I have the same competitive gene. It only takes one comment, like, "I can slide across the kitchen in my socks farther than you can," and boom! The contest begins: juggling tennis balls, balancing a cup on one finger; you name it. It doesn't matter what the challenge is. Competition almost always ensues.

On one family excursion to New York City, we rented bikes to ride through Central Park. When we came up to Columbus Circle, I had the bright idea to let Terry know the race was *on* by smoking past him on my bike. I'm willing to admit that challenging a sixteen-year-old wasn't the wisest thing for a grown man to do, but I told you I'm competitive! He had just started to catch up as the area got more congested, which caused us to ride closer together while pedaling as fast as we could. In an instant, our pedals smacked together, and we both came crashing down in the middle of a mob of people. It was not a pretty sight. Sprawled out and disoriented, we checked to see that we were both still alive and that we hadn't mortally wounded any innocent bystanders. Somehow neither of us or anyone else was hurt or had any broken bones. It was only my pride that had been badly bruised. I felt drenched in the embarrassment of my Bad Dad moment as my wife and daughters shook their heads at us. So, we got back on our bikes and went for the only thing that could soothe a near-death experience: pizza.

We all have some sense of competition that can lead to unhealthy outcomes. An infatuation with competition can create a ripple effect throughout our lives and cause us to move in directions we never intended—like being laid out in the middle of a Central Park crowd. The unhealthy habit of competing with or comparing ourselves to others can suck the life out of our joy; and trying to measure up to other people we think are smarter, more athletic, funnier, or better looking than us *isn't* much fun. It's easy to fall into the trap of feeling like others' agendas, opinions, and actions should shape the way we feel or guide the steps we take. That's why exploring the idea of *freestyling* is so important for me and you.

Traditionally, freestyling has been about improvising activities and interests—such as skateboarding, music, or clothes—on the fly. For example, Bluegrass musician Earl Scruggs will often take classic hits in all kinds of new directions by freestyling musical breaks, and the group Gangstagrass combines the unlikely mashup of bluegrass and rap to create a unique take on each musical genre.

My friend Chad Teague brought new meaning to the word while we were planning a college-reunion weekend. When I gave him an outline for one of the day's activities, he said I shouldn't count him in on my structured itinerary. He was going to be *free-*

styling. Chad told me he wanted to go with *no agenda.* "Just because the world *says* we need a master plan, doesn't mean I do," he explained. Witnessing his willingness to embrace unexpected opportunities was like taking a breath of fresh air we didn't know we needed.

Since then, I've come to embrace freestyling as a simple mindset that suggests we are all in charge of our own lives. We often feel controlled by comparisons we make around money, position, and challenges—all of which can crush our freestyle spirit—and it's easy to get stuck in the mindset that we don't have the ability to embrace unexpected opportunities. We can easily get sucked into the lie that we are prisoners of someone else's agenda. In fact, you may be an actual prisoner as you read this. But I'm here to tell you that you have the option to freestyle your very next steps. Every one of us can freestyle. In the counsel of my friend Henry Cloud, we must remember that "we are all ridiculously in charge of our life and decisions." Yep, if you are alive, breathing, and reading this, then *you*, too, have the freedom to freestyle!

Artists especially understand this kind of freedom. As a student of the "Freedom-to-Freestyle Movement," I love exploring the world of art. I find that going to museums expands my perspective to see that anything is possible. It takes me far beyond the standards I've set for what is normal, what is possible, and what is honorable.

Google *Bicycle Wheel* by Marcel Duchamp and you'll see the work of an artist who thought differently. The piece includes a wheel and a stool constructed in a highly unique way. Duchamp didn't build each of the objects he used in the work. Heck, he didn't even *find* the pieces himself. And yet it sold for $1.2 million over twenty years ago. Think that's irrational? Another one of Duchamp's pieces is recognized by art historians as one of the most influential pieces in modern art. This one titled *Fountain* is an upside-down urinal. What? Is my brain so set on society's definition of beauty that I missed seeing the potential for a urinal to qualify as world-renowned art?

For me, this type of thinking, this idea of playing by your own rules, has the potential to create conversations that expand the walls we've put up for ourselves or that others have built for us. It reminds us that we are *all* free to make beautiful art in life. Freestyling gives us that freedom. A restaurateur can close on the busiest day of the week. A waffle fry cook can write a book. A student can start his own school. A businesswoman can become a full-time mother. A dad can leave work early to be home with his children. A chef can start a food pantry to care for those in need. Large-scale, small-scale, professional, personal, revolutionary, or mundane; at the root of freestyling is the choice, not the action. All you have to do is remember that a potty is a prized piece of art, and then get going.

Wherever you set out to go or whatever you create doesn't have to be perfect. Just getting going can be more about exploring the beauty of the imperfect. Imperfections are terribly wonderful things I love to have conversations about because I, too, am just plain imperfect. Massively imperfect. The Japanese celebrate this idea of imperfect beauty. Wabi-sabi, as they call it, is centered around the acceptance of imperfection. For example, a chipped pottery bowl or one that is not perfectly circular becomes beautiful in its unevenness. Moss growing between rocks takes on a new shade of wonder.

Wabi-sabi provides a fascinating lens through which to look at art, beauty, and life. It's a concept that gives us a fresh way to determine what is pleasing to the senses. You see, looking at life this way means the goal no longer needs to be about achieving perfection in other people's eyes—we can strive to recognize beauty in imperfection instead. Things like art and Wabi-sabi give us the creative liberty to freestyle new paths in life and permission to tear down walls that prevent free thinking so we can find fresh opportunities. Is it easy? Heck no! Is it irrational? Heck yeah!

This out-of-the-box thinking is exactly why I get stoked giving our leadership team subscriptions to *Surfer Magazine*. I've never been surfing, even though I live just hours from the beach. But surfers have a freestyle mentality, and I want to encourage myself and those around me to always think differently about what's possible. These athletes overcome some of the biggest waves Mother Nature throws at them. It takes awesome judgment to select the right wave, and it takes amazing timing to hit it just right; go too early and you get swallowed up, go too late and you miss it altogether. As the waves come rolling in, surfers need both the discipline to follow the rules and the courage to freestyle outside them.

Discipline is as essential for surfing as it is for experiencing freedom in life. Having the discipline to work within individual boundaries and systems is what gives us the flexibility we need to ride the big waves. But hang on one second…Aren't boundaries and systems put in place to keep us boxed in? That's the cool thing about boundaries: we all have the freedom to set our own. You can begin by defining lines you will not cross. Maybe you refuse to tell lies, take on debt, or break the law. Maybe you never want to be overly proud or haughty, discriminate against others, or disrespect their opinions. The list can go on and on! Whatever your boundaries may be, think of them as guardrails set up to protect your path. Imagine that crossing them may negatively impact your ability to freestyle the way you want. It may seem counterintuitive but think of setting boundaries as a way to pave your path to freedom rather than restricting it. Understanding and declaring your boundaries will actually allow you *more* freedom.

Things like addiction, reckless pursuit of instant gratification, and financial debt, for example, are all enemies of freedom. That brand-new, shiny, black car may *look* like freedom, but it suddenly makes you a slave to the banker man when that enormous monthly payment comes due. Having credit card debt can limit the options for your career choices and steal the joy from your desire to be generous toward others. Taking the time to define how you approach what you want versus what you need is a boundary worth exploring. When we start seeing these boundaries as paths to freedom, making the tough decisions becomes rewarding. You may find a sense of power in your rebelliousness by making statements like the following:

"I am keeping my iPhone 6 and you can't stop me."
"I am going to drive my car another year just as it is, and you just have to deal with it."
"Suck on this thought buttercup: I am brewing my own cup of coffee for small group."
"I'll have water instead of soda because I choose to drink from the source of life."

Freestyling is available to anyone and everyone, which serves as a nice reminder that the decisions and paths of other people don't have to look like ours. As a matter of fact, we don't even want them to! We don't want to be the one who steals the joy from another person's journey of self-discovery. Sometimes we stifle people, keeping them in a box and these are folks who need to color outside the lines. What would happen if we all expanded our thinking to allow people to freestyle and be original?

I love the example of when a franchisee presented a problem that he was experiencing in our organization to one of the well-respected executive leaders in our business. The executive leader listened to the franchisee and responded by saying, "Who are you working with on that issue?" After the franchisee explained who he was working with and where they were in the process, the executive simply said, "You're in great hands." That was it. The executive still served as a resource, but he decided not to rob the franchisee of the learning experience or the joy of solving the problem himself. He understood how boundaries can serve as bumpers for growth, and he wanted the franchisee to walk through that experience. Also, he was not going to allow the franchisee's problem to distract him from the important things he was working on.

Similar to setting boundaries, setting up systems in life can create space for our minds to freestyle. You can simplify an activity that feels complicated by building a system to help you understand it and flow through it with more ease. Likewise, creating a structure for a seemingly large or complicated thing gives you space, mentally and organizationally, to examine what it means to *you*. These one-time actions allow more freedom to explore your hopes and dreams in the process.

Early-morning journaling to investigate what the writers of the Bible are telling me, instead of relying on what someone else thinks they are telling me, is a system I have come to utilize regularly in my personal life. Interpreting the readings, however, can feel like a complicated and daunting task. So the structured routine I set up to tackle this challenge resembles some smaller steps: I take a daily walk through the Bible, during which I read a very small section of scripture (I prefer one book at a time and only one to-five verses per day); I then open a document and write the date and verses; and lastly, I simply write how I interpret those few verses and what they mean in my life at that moment. Getting to be vulnerable to yourself is a blast as you record your take on these pages of wisdom. These translations are not for anyone else to read, and the daily discipline ignites my mind to explore God's words as they pertain to me.

A system I use professionally is one we call the "Canton Standard." The system is defined by a series of pictures and ideas that help us set the expectation of excellence specific to *our business* so that we're not crippled by constant comparison. It helps us state, out loud, a commitment to our own standard rather than those set by other businesses. It sets us up to compete against only ourselves; to be our best in whatever areas matter to us.

Let's use the trash can areas in the back of our restaurants as an example. We could constantly send emails to the team about how the area needs to be kept cleaner than clean. Instead, our Canton Standard simply states that we want that area to be "lickable." That's right, we want the trash area to be so clean it's lickable. And to drive the point home, we include a picture of what lickable looks like to us. That way, our team compares the area to the picture and not hundreds of voices or opinions about what *other systems* say it should look like. Then we create a weekly audit of the picture to see if we are following our own standard. The Canton Standard gives us the freedom to set up our systems however and wherever we want; it's a system that prevents us from letting comparison to others steal our joy.

We can set up similar systems for our own lives. I don't have to compare myself to what someone else is doing on any given day and neither do you. Though sometimes understanding the standards of others can help you set your own standard. The examples set by my brother, sister, mom, and dad raise my standards for being a parent and spouse, but they are not my competition. That would be a joy killer. You, too, can create your own standards and hold yourself only to those. This is the key to winning the battle for your freedom. Arm yourself with the tools you need to avoid getting sucked into crossing boundaries that can derail your idea of freedom. Set up a system of shields that will help you push back comparisons to others.

My son Terry is one of my favorite freestylers. Due to some poor family choices his biological parents made, he had a tough childhood and was taken into foster care at ten years old. He suddenly found himself separated from his three sisters, all of whom ended up in different homes. While this caused unbelievable hardship for all of them, Terry was a boy whose personality beamed with kindness and optimism. When Terry entered our home at the age of thirteen, he was separated from everything he had ever known and was plopped down in the middle of our three daughters, who were nine, twelve, and fourteen at the time.

The following years were some of the hardest and the greatest we've known as a family. Adjusting to the way adoption changes life in an instant is a tremendous challenge. Terry, and everyone in our family, was being asked to change their whole life and go on like it was just another day. There was no script to follow or outcome to guarantee. We all needed the courage to step into the world of freestyling, and thankfully, we could see that it would be worth it. Now, if we gave this transition space, bringing Terry into our family would also be a tremendous joy. His youthfulness, humor, and energy shined a wonderful light into our lives.

We wanted our son to be the best version of himself, and that meant we would have to be the best version of ourselves as parents. That meant we would have to retool ourselves to forge new parental skills that would allow us all a little wiggle room. If, by mistake, we got lured into making comparisons to or evaluating our success against other parents, we would miss the complexity of the person God created Terry to be. Having a flexible approach helped our family take the spotlight off our own expectations and highlight the beauty of serving another person. It helped us have the courage to keep moving forward, to always lead with love, and to take small steps together every day. Our persevering as a family through something that is easy to start but hard to finish was freestyling at its finest.

Reflecting on those days, I recently asked Terry, who is now in his twenties, how he coped with the challenges he faced growing up. He said something we can all learn from: "I just felt the next day was going to be better." Having hope for tomorrow is what freedom feels like.

If you want to feel free, know that you are free—free to be you. My friend Chad gave this idea to me and I am giving it to you: keep freestyling. Don't let the world's standards and agenda or another's opinion steal your freedom. Let this wisdom allow you to irrationally dial down judgment and crank up an appreciation for originality. Stride free and easy knowing that a large-minded God has made and blessed all things. Go after the things you love and let them take you on an infinite road trip to destinations above and beyond your wildest dreams. Let *Surfer Magazine* and the art of Marcel Duchamp serve as reminders that we can contribute to the Freedom-to-Freestyle Movement that's racing across the globe. Go ahead. Go forth and make art out of urinals.

KINDNESS PAUSE

What is a spontaneous thing you could do today?
Name a scenario where you often feel stuck, but you now
realize you could freestyle?

CHAPTER 8

CERTIFIED SIGNATURE MOVE

"I want to think of myself as a human being.
Under the sky, under the heavens, there is but one family.
It just so happens that people are different."
- Bruce Lee

Once upon a time, I asked a girl on a date to see the famous Broadway play *Cats* at the Fox Theater in Atlanta. This girl had been my friend for several years, but it became more for me suddenly one day. She was heading off on a trip and asked if I could pick her up at the airport when she returned home. I gladly said I would and told her I was excited she'd selected me. Then weird things started happening while she was out of town. I started to miss her! I began feeling jealous and afraid she might meet a new guy while she was away.

Immediately, I started counting the days until she returned. On the night of her arrival, I waited and waited for a call that never came. By then I was in full-blown jealous mode, already heartbroken and filled with a sense of urgency; I had to get this girl on an official date *stat!*

I called her the next day. She explained she'd had one of her roommates pick her up because she didn't want to bother me. Love is weird, isn't it? She was completely oblivious to the harrowing emotional trauma I'd experienced while she was gone. Of course, I didn't tell her. I simply expressed that I'd been excited about picking her up. Then I told her I wanted to take her on an official date. Low and behold, she accepted!

We'd previously gone on many friendly adventures that were like dates but definitely not dates, so I was pumped to pick her up for our first *real* date. When the play began, dozens of people dressed in cat outfits filled the stage with dancing and singing. The music was beautiful and relaxing. It was so relaxing that about halfway through the show, nestled in my seat, I hit the snooze button. I dozed in and out of some of the best sleep I'd had since I was a baby.

It wasn't the first time I'd fallen asleep somewhere embarrassing, and it wouldn't be the last. To this day I have a tendency to fall asleep in meetings and training sessions. In doing so, I've learned that people often love to take pictures of me or point out my repose to others seated nearby in a chorus of whispers. I've come to expect it.

I was refreshed when I woke up toward the end of the play, but I quickly realized this was probably not the best move for a first date. I hoped—as I do every time I grab a quick snooze—no one had noticed. I thought perhaps she was so into the dancing cats that she never looked over to notice *my* little cat nap. But I couldn't risk it. I confessed to her that I'd fallen asleep and quickly added that it was some of the most refreshing, happy sleep I'd ever had.

Then my date did something amazing, something so surprising I carved it into my brain so I can still remember it perfectly more than twenty-five years later. She didn't show me a picture that she took of me sleeping through the show. She didn't ask me rudely how I could fall asleep during this expensive, world-renowned production. She didn't get mad, explain how much I missed, or suggest that I should be ashamed of myself. Not for a second. Weirdly, she was genuinely excited that I enjoyed the play exactly the way I did. She said she was just happy we were together.

This is why I instantly fell in love with Gwen, big time. She gave me space to be myself. She understood my style, and she didn't let it annoy her. She embraced my signature move, and she earned my official seal of approval—my certified signature. She was grade A and without a doubt someone I wanted to be around a long time. Lucky for me, we're married now.

I could see then that Gwen was an original, and I love originals.

Even if I've never met you, there's one thing I know about you for sure: You're 100 percent original, just like Gwen. You are the best you in the entire world. You are a child of God. There has never been another you, and there never will be. Every person is an original.

I'm often blown away when I see individuals doing the amazing things only they can do; things I can only dream of doing. Take Chris Rock, for example. He is one of the funniest people I've ever seen, and he can crack up a crowd simply by walking on stage. Or Alicia Keys, a beautiful musician with a smile that can light up the world. Rosa Parks stood up to injustice with a sense of bravery I could only aspire to possess. Elton John combines a heart for social change with musical artistry that astounds me.

Each of these artists and activists is amazing at their craft and they shine brightest by showcasing their distinct talents and unique personalities for the world to enjoy. But give you and me some time, and we can surely do some things they can't. Like my sensei A.L. Patterson teaches when it comes to being you, no one can compare. He proudly says, "I am the best there ever was at being me."

Be your own biggest cheerleader in life! When was the last time you told yourself that you are freaking amazing? If you need reminding, write a note to yourself and put it on the mirror so you can read it daily.

Only you can be you because God designed you. He knows how many hairs are on your head. And He has a plan for you. So, don't let the world tell you what you should be, and don't be intimidated by those who want to put you in a box. Find what's original about you and surround yourself with people who appreciate it. The world needs me and you to be at our unique best. That is when we add the most value—not when we try to be like someone else or constantly compare ourselves to others. That's a killjoy and a time suck.

Remember what a guy named Paul wrote to his friends in Galatia. Let it remind you to "make a careful exploration of who you are and the work you have been given, and then sink yourself into that. Don't be impressed with yourself. Don't compare yourself with others. Each of you must take responsibility for doing the creative best you can with your own life."

I've spent my life exploring objects, places, hobbies, and ideas that I connect with, and that are 100 percent original. As I come across these things I treasure, I mentally mark them as approved with a "certified signature." I stamp them as top-grade, choice-cut, USDA-registered originals. This marks them as things that I love, want to shine a light on, and whimsically share with others. They are things that exude quality and excellence. They are creative things I want to be associated with to help me as I strive to learn and grow.

There is something special about declaring something with your certified signature, whether it's a person you like, a piece of art you admire, or a move only you can do. It's fun to announce aloud that *this* is my certified signature move. Keep in mind, falling asleep in public isn't my only signature move. Another one of my signatures revolves around my love for great socks. If nothing else, my socks serve as a reminder that God sees me— and my feet—as beautiful when I "sock-up" each day.

Over the years, I've relied on different companies for my certified signature socks. The coolest thing about having a certified signature move is that you get to decide what it is *and* make changes to it whenever you want! Right now, my favorite sock brand is a company called Stance. I never start a day without putting on a pair of Stance socks. The company is bold enough to say that they exist to celebrate human originality. It may sound peculiar and ridiculous to some, but it's ideal for me; this is what I want from my socks. They fit perfectly and they give me the power kickstart to each new day. One day I hope to partner with Stance and design my own pair of socks, an *Irrational Kindness* edition. I've shared this dream, as well as a design idea, with the customer service representatives at Stance, but they haven't taken me up on it...yet.

Years ago, I started collecting stockpiles of socks to share with friends. I could fill a warehouse with the socks I've secured over the years! The routine goes like this: I build up a supply of socks and then sit down and decide which socks pair with which person in my life. I write a note to remind whomever I choose that he or she is hand-crafted by God. When the socks go in the mail, my prayer is for each recipient to feel loved by their creator—and by me.

I have learned that one of the best ways to own your originality, your own certified signatures, is to say out loud the characteristics you want to claim with your life. Calling out these traits (such as compassion or generosity) is an exercise in uncomplicating things. You're simply stating what you value and what is uniquely you. This practice is critical for any employee, business leader, entrepreneur, and all-around humans because it makes you hold yourself accountable for what is most important to you. Saying aloud what you want to be known for is also great because it gives you a mental imprint so that you can always refer to it.

For example, we have a rather irrational signature we seek to own often at our Chick-fil-A restaurants in Canton. Ready for it? It's *failure*. Yep, in addition to touting kindness as being of the utmost importance, we say out loud that failing is an approved signature move in our organization. And we do it so that when we fail in any capacity it is *embraced* as a job well done. We want to make team members feel safe enough to take some risks. The way we see it, we would rather restrain mustangs than kick mules. We cannot very well call out kindness as the beacon by which we want to be known and simultaneously reprimand someone for failing. If we did, neither kindness nor failure would be true signature moves, would they?

For instance, let's say we have a team member who, without permission, gives away a meal to a guest who forgot his wallet. If we get upset with that team member, it stands in contrast to our belief of showing *irrational* kindness. If we instruct our team members to do the job they were told to do, and nothing more, then we are not fully inviting them to experience a bigger adventure. If we didn't welcome failure, we would miss the opportunity to seek new ideas or discover the unique heart and compassion each team member brings to our organization.

Now for a true story: One evening I was offering drink refills to guests in the dining room when I approached a table where a man and his daughter were seated. The young girl was holding a piece of scrap paper in her hands and wearing a smile that stretched ear to ear. The father shared with me that he loved our team and explained what had made his daughter so happy. It turned out that one of our team members, Cooper, had given the girl a handwritten note that she could use to redeem a free ice cream cone, which she was also invited to make herself.

We didn't have coupons like this, but Cooper had taken it upon himself to create a handmade coupon with his own pen—a Cooper Coupon for a free Icedream cone and a VIP pass to hand-make it in our kitchen. His signature move was risky. Not only could he have been rejected by the guest, but he also could have gotten in trouble for giving away the cost of an Icedream cone. When we lift up kindness and failure together as certified signature moves, we give our team space to discover their own unique ways to live out these characteristics we value. When we choose to lift up stories that highlight the heroic actions of our team members and each other, it raises our values too and holds us accountable to them. It makes our core competency kindness, day in and day out.

We could see the power of Cooper's signature move in action when the girl came behind the counter to make her own Icedream cone. When someone announced that she was training to become a future team member, cheers erupted from all our team members. If that young girl does come to work for us, it will be because she always remembered the kindness that Cooper showed her in that moment. If we had proclaimed profit as our restaurant's signature move, then you can bet Cooper would never have offered that family the unique experience they enjoyed so much. But he knew that showing kindness even in the face of possible failure was a signature move we sought to embrace.

So, think about it. What are your certified signature moves? Say them out loud. Say them proud. Proclaim what you love and who you want to be to all who will listen. Embrace your idiosyncrasies. These traits are distinctively *you* and they can be magnified by God in unbelievable ways. Find a source of energy in all the things you love. Shine each one as English theologian and evangelist John Wesley suggested: "Do all the good you can, by all the means you can, in all the ways you can, in all the places you can, at all the times you can, to all the people you can, as long as you ever can."

We are unique individuals who can walk alongside each other and celebrate our unique certified signature moves rather than compare them. We can move together in the same direction *and* in opposite directions, always leaving just enough space to be ourselves and to let others do the same. Half the fun is identifying them out loud to yourself. The other half is sharing them with others. I can't wait to see what you come up with!

If you want to have "restful meditation," I suggest you go see *Cats*. Oh, and if Stance ever grants me a "Cooper Coupon" to personally design my own socks, you better believe I'm gonna send everyone a pair with KINDNESS written boldly across the tops. A guy can dream, can't he?

KINDNESS PAUSE

What is your signature color?
If it were a paint sample, what would you name it?

CHAPTER 9

MY BIG TOE

*"One of the most difficult things is not to change society—
but to change yourself."*
- Nelson Mandela

Let me tell you about my big toe. It is a gift from God! My parents told me that when I was a few days old, I somehow managed to rub off my big toenail on the side of my crib. It was there until one day it wasn't, and then my toe looked a mess. Thankfully, the nail eventually grew back, but it looked more like a turtle shell than a toenail. I apologize upfront for the picture this may leave in your mind, and I could tell you about the joy of using wire cutters to clip this indestructible toenail but that would border on disgusting. So, let me just say this: If God needed a stronger material to secure the walls of Fort Knox, he could absolutely duplicate whatever he used to reconstruct my big toe.

There were times when I felt insecure about this strange part of me, and I often opted to wear sneakers over flip-flops in the summertime. Until one day, while visiting my grandparents Papa and Grandmother, I encountered an unexpected sight that changed everything I ever thought about my toe—and about life.

After a long workday, Papa took off his shoes, and I saw his feet for the first time. And what did I see? He had a toenail just like mine! I couldn't believe that I had never realized my grandfather had the same messed up, funky, big toe.

Seeing Papa's toe changed something in me; something I once thought was awful had suddenly turned into something way cool. My big toe was no longer an embarrassing deformity, but a toe of which I could be proud because Papa had the same one. After all, he was a role model to me; he was a man I admired and wanted to emulate.

You see, Papa and Grandmother were farmers and they were always inviting me to the farm for adventures. Papa wore a hat and overalls almost every day of his life—except for Sundays—and sported the most perfect farmer's tan you have ever seen. He was up before the sun and worked until the cows came home. Papa only completed schooling up until the fifth grade and Grandmother the eighth grade, but to me, they were the smartest folks in the world.

I always thought Papa had the perfect life. He was kind, he loved his family and his community, and he had a laugh that could cheer up a whole room. When I learned about his past, however, I realized he had to work very hard to become the man I so admired.

Over time, I learned Papa was no stranger to adversity. It all began with his dad, Henry, who was also a farmer and an entrepreneur, but one who had an alcohol problem. During his so-called one-man parties, he would spiral into dark two- and three-day periods of excessive drinking and binge to the point of passing out in his chair at the dinner table. This is the father figure by whom my weird-toed Papa was raised. In many ways, Papa was forced to parent his own father. Sometimes, he would secretly unhook the coils of his father's truck and hide them so Henry would be unable to drive until he was sober. Other times, Papa would seek out his father's stash of moonshine and smash the jugs with a hammer so Henry couldn't consume the contents.

Having grown up during the Great Depression in rural Georgia, Papa found himself working full-time on a farm at the age of eleven. Personally, I can't imagine sending my children to work forty-hour weeks at that age, when I was still trying to get them to clean their rooms and empty the cat litter box. I was probably wise to let them continue with middle school, especially since truancy laws are different today, but the world was a different place in 1921.

Back then Papa grew up working, fell in love with a woman named Ida, whom he married and with whom he had his first baby. Tragically, Ida never made it out of the hospital due to complications with the birth of their son. At the age of twenty-one, Papa became a single parent to a newborn named Edgar. He met Mary, my grandmother, a couple of years later and they were married shortly thereafter. Before long, they, too, were pregnant and gave birth to their first-born child. Billy died at only nine months old. By the age of twenty-five, Papa had already experienced financial hardship, a limited education, an alcoholic father, and the death of his first wife and second-born son. That kind of start to life could have set the stage for a failure mindset. It would have been easy for him to focus so narrowly on his shame that he would miss the opportunity for better.

And yet Papa, who was clearly swamped by adversity from the start, translated those challenges into kindness toward himself and others. He had every reason to dwell on his difficult circumstances, to be bitter and resentful, but he chose to follow a path paved by hard work and love instead. His faith in God especially helped give him a different perspective; it reminded him that he was living for something more than just himself.

Church was the anchor of Papa's life. Each Sunday, he let farming take a back seat to church, where he could be found rain or shine. Apart from feeding the animals, Papa set Sundays aside specifically for worship. He was an active deacon in his church and took a lot of pride in how he looked on Sunday mornings. He taught his children that on Sunday you put on your very best clothes and go to church with dignity. Appearance was important to my grandmother too, but she found the most joy in preparing amazing Sunday meals. She would beam while presenting them to the family and watching everyone enjoy her feasts.

Helping others in their own ways was a source of strength for my grandparents. I can easily recall hearing many stories about their love for the community and witnessing it first-hand. Papa once got up at midnight and used his tractor to help a neighbor get his car out of a ditch. He and Grandmother invited one of his brothers, his wife, and two children to come live with them when one of them was sick. They took in two more family members when a sister of theirs developed terminal cancer, and they cared for her and her husband until her death. They invited aging grandparents to live with them through different seasons of their lives. In each instance, Papa seemed to have a double helping of kindness that was so reassuring that people just knew he was going to take care of them.

Papa's foundation in genuine love allowed him to challenge others to strive for more than mediocrity. One of his primary objectives was to see all three of his sons—Edgar, Jimmy, and Don—receive college educations. He frequently talked to them about the importance of having the formal education he was never fortunate enough to receive. My dad, Jimmy, can remember with clarity the happiness on Papa's face when he started college his freshman year. It was clear Papa refused to let his limited education stand in his way of all three of his sons eventually graduating from the University of Georgia. (Go Dawgs!)

Instead, he and Grandmother met hard times head-on by adapting to life's challenges. Change was something they had learned to embrace because they had to. To them change was, and still is, one of life's guarantees. When the economy shifted, they adjusted from growing row-crops of corn and cotton to raising chickens. They adjusted to life after losing a second child, Charles, who died of meningitis when he was nine. My grandparents, who were together twenty-four seven, adjusted together in life. They chose time and again to leave arguments and disagreements behind and to focus instead on lifting up others—and each other—however they could.

We have a choice too. We can choose to be held hostage by our circumstances—our mistakes, the nightly news, toxic relationships, unexpected tragedies—or we can change our perspective from one focused on insurmountable adversity to one focused on hope, inspiration, and opportunity. What makes all the difference is the perspective we have about the problem at hand, no matter how big or small. It determines how we respond to the challenge and how we treat others when we do.

Your life could certainly be filled with even greater tragedies and challenges than those my Papa faced. Yet with perseverance and perspective, we all have opportunities to turn stories riddled with devastation, anger, and grief into beautiful tales of impact. We can each approach the start of a new day holding tight to the belief that what we do with that day matters and for far longer than we can imagine. One of the greatest lessons I learned from my Papa, and hope to pass along, is that you don't have to have every detail of your life planned out in front of you for it to be a success. The first step is simply believing that today is enough. We have a chance today to start anew. Every day we get to have an entirely new outlook on life and the challenges it deals us.

This hopeful perspective won't likely prove to be a quick fix, just as the adjustments my Papa made to his life's challenges were not quick fixes. His sadness almost surely felt insurmountable at times. However, he chose to take the high road of irrational kindness instead of getting mired down with bitterness and resentment, and you can too!

You may be struggling with your own challenges such as dealing with peer pressure, low self-esteem, changing relationships, hiring decisions, or a recent loss—to the point that it feels suffocating at times. Sometimes, it's easy to believe the myth that we are the only one in the world facing the problems or struggles we do. We see someone who is successful and think they must never have been subject to any of the challenges we have been, yet without knowing their reality or history. We can become fixated on the bad weather in our lives. When what matters more than the bad weather is where you're heading in the midst of the storm. And you don't have to just suck it up, buttercup! Rather, realize this adversity is the *fuel to find the cool.* Go ahead and wear those flip-flops and show off that nasty big toe.

There is a line in the book of Isaiah that reads, "How beautiful are the feet of those that bring the good news." I love this verse because we rarely think of feet as being beautiful (exhibit A right here!), yet God sees something so much more; he sees a Van Gogh painting. He sees that you have a message of hope to bring to the world even, and perhaps especially, amid the most difficult parts of your journey. The adversity you're facing is helping to create a captivating story of impact for future generations. It may not be easy to see at first because this way of thinking can present many buts. You may say to yourself—

"But my superior doesn't think that way."

"But my friend is so messed up."

"But he promised."

"But what's going on in the world is freaking me out, and there's nothing I can do."

"But she hates me."

"But I have no idea how to change my situation."

"But I'm not good enough."

To those we say: life's journey is not a sprint. Your job is just to start somewhere, from wherever you are, and move your focus off the problem toward a new way of thinking, informed by your faith. And remember also, to give yourself some grace. If ever you feel unsure of where to go, look down at your feet—Not mine, please! I have a heinous toe—and recognize the opportunity you have to start today.

Cat Stevens sings, "But take your time, think a lot, why, think of everything you've got." In the fast-food industry, we have constant reminders in our business of the pains of inadequacy, failure, stuckness, hurriedness, and how impossible it is to hoard buckets of joy to use at your leisure. Practice finding joy and gratitude in the truth that today is a new day to serve and grow. It changes everything when we realize that Eden is ahead of us, not behind us.

When it feels all too easy to be cynical and stay locked in your struggles, think of Papa. We can look at his early life and see crushed dream after crushed dream. But what if we viewed Papa's life the way God sees it—as beautiful? What if we cultivated an attitude of adaptability and caring for others, just like Papa did? What if we looked down at our feet, at our broken stories, and said, "I have the chance to bring good news, no matter what my imperfection."

The awesome thing about seeing our adversity the way God sees it is that it takes the pressure off us. It takes the focus off our situation and it allows us to have faith that we are right where God wants us—even if that place is in the middle of the storm.

And when it seems impossible, remember that you're just getting started on a new path. Don't look back or let your dreams get paralyzed by what the cynics tell you. Let love rule and create a story with faith in tomorrow. When it would be easier to let adversity shape you, whittle out some space for irrational kindness in your life. After all, the next generation needs you. Just like I needed my Papa and his beautifully weird big toe.

KINDNESS PAUSE

What makes life hard for you today?
What is a next step you can take to make tomorrow better?

CHAPTER 10

MY HERO

---

*"Live an example, so that if your children do the same things
you do, you would be proud of them."*
- Jim and Barbara Williams

"You can't let this die."

As soon as my staff member, Alex Gomez, declared these words to me, they were etched into my mind forever. He said it in response to an obstacle we had run into after my friend, Howard Cox, challenged Chick-fil-A to take part in the MUST Ministries summer lunch program for a day, which fed 5,000 underprivileged children in Atlanta. Every day countless volunteers mobilized like clockwork to hand out meals to hungry children across seven counties—no doubt a monumental task.

Now, don't get me wrong. I love taking on big, impactful, electrifying ideas that seem destined to crash and burn. However, this challenge was like a spectacular, unplanned, foreign dream that hit me with the same rush and overwhelm as trying to uncover Guthrie's secret sauce. It was one of those ideas that had the potential to inspire people all over to climb a mountain or sail across a stormy sea; it was one of those things that would go down in history.

To make it even more challenging, the program could not be fulfilled through a corporate initiative. It had to be done by pooling together more than forty individual business owners who could agree to align on one single idea. We would need independent franchisees to commit their time, employees, food, and energy—much of which was already being directed toward other, pre-planned initiatives—to this program. But if we could take over the program for a day over the summer, it would mean that five thousand children who regularly found peanut butter sandwiches in their bags would receive a hot Chick-fil-A sandwich meal, delivered by "cows" and our team, right to their homes.

After working on the idea for months, I realized coupling the logistical struggles with our own restaurant challenges would be too much to overcome. It was just too difficult to get 100 percent of the people on board, while they were knee-deep in the busyness of their own restaurants, to actually pull off this dream. Moving forward would mean requiring some franchisees to deliver food to areas that were not even in the community they served. It would mean some franchisees would have to invite other franchisees into their territory, where, by competitive nature, they feel protective. It would mean some franchisees could have to forgo their already-planned donations to organizations and schools with whom they may have had stronger connections. It was going to require so many exhausting, one-on-one conversations to rally everyone around the vision. I wanted everyone around me to magically read my mind and jump on board without going through the healthy, necessary process of facing adversity when trying something big.

I can still clearly see myself the day I walked into the office at our Riverstone Parkway location to tell Alex the bad news. I was standing in the doorway with Alex seated at the desk when I began explaining to him that the program was just too big a hurdle to clear. That's when he looked me in my eyes and said the words that would change me forever: "You can't let this die."

The mission was much more personal for Alex. He was four years old and living in Mexico when his father was fatally electrocuted in an accident at a hotel dry-cleaner where he worked. Because of the family's impoverished circumstances, his mother was forced to find another way to support the family. So shortly after losing her husband, she immigrated to the United States, leaving Alex and his siblings behind. He lived with his elderly grandmother in unrelenting hardship and only saw his mom a few times over the next ten years. He recalls pulling old gum off telephone poles just to have something to chew. I can only imagine how hard that must be for anyone, let alone such a young boy.

Then at fifteen years old, Alex and his brother made the trek from Mexico to Northern California, where their mother was working. He remembered feeling both helpless because he couldn't speak English and happy to be reunited with his mom. Because the family was still experiencing extreme financial hardship, often sleeping in their car, the brothers went to work to help earn money. They took the only jobs they felt qualified to take, and they worked long hours picking vegetables in the hot California fields. Alex's hands and body often hurt so badly; the pain almost pushed him to the point of passing out. But he didn't complain; he was so elated to regain lost time with his mom and contribute financially to his family.

When he wasn't working in the fields, Alex took classes to learn English as a second language. Because his mother taught the family that education was the only way to advance, he saw the lessons as a pathway to growth and success. And as soon as he got an opportunity, Alex enrolled in an adult literacy program and successfully completed his GED.

I met Alex—and the signature, voluminous ponytail that trailed down his back—when he and his brother Fidel walked into our restaurant. It was 1998 and, having already lived in the United States for seven years, they moved to Georgia in the footsteps of some family members who had found work here. Alex was intrigued by the idea of working with a company that would risk losing so much money by being closed on Sunday. I offered him and his brother a job, but I told Alex that he would have to cut off his ponytail. He was quick to communicate that his ponytail was his source of energy. To him, it was a Superman cape, Batman accessory belt, and a Wonder Woman lasso, all combined into one cord of dazzling beauty. Cutting it off would be his kryptonite. He insisted he could magically make it disappear under his hat so I would never see it. He proved it to me, and, with this understanding, we agreed that Alex and his ponytail would join the team.

By some standards, Alex was not a shooting star. He spoke terrible English. He was quiet. He was not wildly confident in his direction. But as I got to know Alex, he unveiled another superpower that radiated as bright as the sun; it was that he saw every day as a new opportunity. What he didn't have, he made up for with a bright smile, a solid work ethic, an unwavering commitment to serving others, and most importantly, a spirit of embracing improvement. I was inspired just by observing Alex because he never took a day off from *trying to be a better person*. While he saw himself as coming into Chick-fil-A for a job to get a paycheck, I saw Alex in a totally different light. I looked at him as a guy who, despite having been through so much, was just getting started on his journey in life. And he had a belief in a better day. That is the key to greatness, and who doesn't want to hang around people like that?

This is why it means something when Alex Gomez looks you in the eyes and tells you to not give up. Recalling his poverty as a young boy, he was reflecting on just how much a hot Chick-fil-A sandwich would have meant to him when he was a child. Here was someone with street cred basically telling me to stop being such a namby-pamby; here was someone with grit telling me not to quit at the first two, three, or even twenty bumps in the road. Alex was watching the fight from my corner and he was telling me not to leave the ring yet. He could see through a different lens, and every story has the power to change when we seek to look through each other's lenses.

So, we dug back in, and at 11 a.m. on July 16, 2014, forty different franchisees, with hundreds of team members and their "cows," delivered over five thousand meals across Atlanta. In the years since then, the number has swelled to feeding ten thousand hungry children annually. But, by God's grace, we've been able to serve them all on one day each summer.

Alex no longer has his ponytail, but he now leads our restaurants as Director of Operations and manages more than three hundred team members. He didn't achieve success through a quick, bright, shooting-star-like rise to fame, but rather as a result of his slow-burning persistence. He continued taking steps toward getting better every day, furthering his education, and investing in his community by teaching English and talking to school groups about his story.

Working with Alex, and many others, has taught me to see people not as who they are now, but who they can become in the future. You see, you don't have to have all the answers about where folks are going in life. Just invest time in caring enough to offer a vision of where they *could be* or where they *might go* someday. They don't need you to map out every step of the way and you shouldn't take it personally if they don't take a step you suggest. Just stand alongside them and continue encouraging them on their journey. In doing so, we are simply offering to take the next step together with them.

Providing them with this encouragement and support means you're jumping onto the path they're clearing and swinging the machete with them. It is an intentional decision to understand that joy is found by pouring time and energy into other people so you can give them a boost on their journey. It's a way to get the joy, joy, joy, joy down in my heart, to stay. It's an attitude shift from thinking about how people can serve me to how I can serve them. Because when I start caring as much about the hearts and paths of others as I do my own, then *my* joy increases. It's a Jedi mind trick on joy; serving others serves our own hearts.

Offering encouragement is one of the simplest ways we can serve others, and every one of us can do it at any time. Encouragement can take the form of inviting someone for a cup of coffee to talk about their hopes and dreams or going to see the play they're in at school. It can be as simple as smiling at or saying hello to someone at school you don't normally engage with. You could share a podcast that meant something to you with a friend or surprise them with a book. You could write six encouraging letters a week, and at the end of the year, you would have loved three hundred more people a year. Don't have three hundred stamps? Then you could call six people a week, encouraging three hundred in a year via phone. Boom. And all of this works best if you can focus on offering encouraging words rather than giving instructions. Start by shifting your mind to focus on serving others and then let God whisper wisdom into the opportunities.

I don't do this right all the time, and I miss all kinds of opportunities whenever I get blinded by my own dreams, busyness,
and responsibilities. But don't let the overwhelming idea of serving
everybody cause you to miss the adventure of serving *someone*. And
don't get bummed if you get burned. Don't get hung up if one person takes advantage of your generosity. Just dust yourself off and
keep going! Seek the risk and reward of loving a world that may
not love you back. When you open your eyes each morning, put on
your irrational pants, and saddle back up.

For irrational kindness to work, you must learn to be okay with
an unbalanced scale. It won't be fair, but *it is okay* not to get back
every single thing we put into a relationship. We're not in charge
of both sides of the equation; we just have to handle *our side* of the
deal because it's the only thing we have any control over. The good
news is that if you focus on your end of the equation in greater
numbers, then you turn a plus sign into a multiplication sign. Your
power to encourage others can grow exponentially.

In the workplace, this encouragement doesn't come without
expectations. In fact, just the opposite. I clearly explain to all our
new Chick-fil-A team members that they will be challenged to give
their best since we believe people *rise* to meet the challenges set
before them. If we set the bar low, we don't give them a margin to
grow. Telling them just to "be on time and do what we tell you,"
suggests they are simply a commodity that is there to serve us. Yet
when we offer them a bigger, more challenging way of thinking
about their jobs, it opens up more space for them to pour creativity
and passion into their work. We remind new hires that they are the
freshest eyes in our organization, and we need their input to continue improving. We want their job to lend them opportunities to
learn, grow, and —yep— even *fail* on our dime. In my experience,
people accept new challenges more readily and wind up perform-

ing better than expected when they are encouraged and supported.

In Alex's case, challenging him meant recognizing his goals and encouraging his dream of pursuing a college degree. It required more than just sharing my knowledge about college with him. It meant going further and getting in the car with him, visiting campuses, and helping him understand the obstacles, the requirements, and the costs. Every second turned out to be worth it when Alex was recognized as the top student on his college graduation day. This is what he shared when he spoke to the entire faculty and graduating class:

"As I said before, no one is more surprised to be here right now than me. As a child growing up in Mexico, without my father or mother, I had many dreams. But I never even dreamed I might get the opportunity, someday, to serve as an ambassador for college education in the United States.

My father will not be here to witness this moment. But my son will. He is the same age—four years old—as I was when I lost my father. I know that my father's memory and my son's love will always encourage me to perform at my best.

Everybody has dreams. Everybody deserves a chance to reach their dreams. Today, I am achieving one of my dreams. I dream my story will make a difference in the lives of my children. I dream that my story will make a difference in the lives of everyone who faces difficult obstacles."

The trust and encouragement I offered Alex came back to me tenfold when my community multiplied on the stage that day.

Now he's not just an inspiration to me, but also the entire city of Canton, Georgia. In fact, the Mayor and City Council officially declared May 17th as Alex Gomez Day and recognized him with a key to the city. You'd better believe we celebrate each year by loading up with Alex's favorite things. To us, it's bigger than any holiday on the calendar. Okay maybe not Christmas, but it crushes Halloween.

Having irrational kindness is about going on a journey together and lifting each other up. Don't judge a book by its cover, a song by its title, or people by who they are today. Tell them you'll make room for their ponytail, their different language, and their unique story. Then start walking alongside them, creating space in which they can grow, fail, and achieve their dreams. The best part is that you don't have to have all the answers as a friend, co-worker, or parent. You don't have to have all the answers when you hire new folks. Because you never know what kind of adventure lies ahead! Seize the unexpected opportunities to be generous—with your time, your words of encouragement, and your belief in others.

Is it difficult to have this mindset? Yes. Will it give you heartburn sometimes? Yes. But will you impact lives in ways you can't even dream up? Yes! So, let me tell you what my hero told me: You can't let this die!

KINDNESS PAUSE

Call someone and tell them why you think they're awesome.

CHAPTER 11

AREN'T YOU GLAD?

*"If you look through history, all the big changes in society
have been started by people at the grassroots level,
people like you and me."*
- Greta Thunberg

I love John Mellencamp. We could talk about just him and his rock 'n' roll career for the remainder of the book and it would be amazing. His life has so many great stories, including the one about how his record company didn't care for his last name so they decided he should be John Cougar. Turned out Mellencamp was not a fan of the new name. (I personally would have loved it! If I could pull off Kevin Cougar, I would in a heartbeat, but unfortunately, I am not that cool.) But cool John Cougar just waited until he gained so much influence that no one dared stop him when he changed his name back.

That's just one of about 124 different reasons why I love him.

In fact, I love him so much that one weekend in my early twenties, my friend Bret Garwood and I decided it was time to meet him. Now, if by some chance you don't know who singer/songwriter John Mellencamp is, just insert the name of your favorite musician here instead. Imagine wanting to meet Taylor Swift, Kendrick Lamar, Beyoncé, or Yo-Yo Ma, and imagine *that* is what it was like for me to go find John Mellencamp. Bret and I figured if you want to meet someone, then you should just get in a car and go see them.

So, with very little money in our pockets, we began our quest to go say hello to the superstar one Friday after work. Imitating the adventure of "Jack and Diane," we spent the next several days driving around rural Indiana on a free-form scavenger hunt. We knocked on his parents' door. We met his aunt at her roller-skating rink. We ate at the drive-up diner we heard he frequented. We came close, but we never found him. It would most likely have been an uncomfortable, awkward, stalkerish situation if we had met him, but, hey, it was worth a shot! Through this experience and many others, I've found it's more fun to come *close* to success than to never have tried in the first place.

One of my favorite things in life is watching people who dream big and pursue those dreams. Although, the thing about dreams is that there's rarely any guarantee they can be accomplished. Sometimes dreams are loftier than can be accomplished in this lifetime, and oftentimes, our dreams are totally preposterous! But what kind of lives would we have without them? Aren't you glad there are people who dream, who make an attempt to change the world, even when they don't know exactly *how* they'll do it?

Aren't you glad there are people like Truett Cathy, who set out to build a successful restaurant business, yet chose to close on Sundays so employees could have a day to rest? Aren't you glad there are people like Dr. Martin Luther King, Jr., who stood up against racial hatred with a persistent yet non-violent approach? Aren't you glad there are people like Mother Theresa, who devoted herself to working among the poorest slums of Calcutta armed with only a passion at first? Aren't you glad there are people like Chance the Rapper, who pours his life into youth and minority communities and uses his talent and fame to provide resources for the arts in the Chicago Public School system? Aren't you glad there are people like Boyan Slat, who at eighteen began the world's largest clean-up project and started the daunting journey to purge the Pacific Ocean of plastic? I sure am.

The one thing they had in common was that they dreamed above and beyond what they knew they could accomplish, and they took steps toward achieving those dreams. They had dreams, but they didn't know how they would turn out. They took a chance and banked on bright days ahead, not knowing how the adventure would end. They embraced the possibility of incredible failure— and this approach inspires our entire team in Canton, Georgia.

Our journey in dreaming bigger began when we started searching for a new meeting space. For years, we had used the crowded Chick-fil-A dining room as our meeting space, complete with all the distractions and buzzing activity that comes with serving guests. When we were desperate for quiet, we would partner with local banks and businesses that allowed us to use their meeting rooms. We eventually graduated to sharing a space with the Goshen Valley Boys Ranch that could hold ten to fifteen people, yet the opportunity to one day have our own space to have these meetings was something we always dreamed of. Knowing it would be a huge asset to our team, we began the process of finding the perfect location.

After months of searching, I drove past a small church with a for-sale sign in the front yard. I didn't even know you could *buy* a church, but here was one for sale. It immediately stoked a new vision for a potential space where the whole community could gather. We imagined teaching financial classes to youth, hosting school events, and leadership conferences. Our minds raced with so many possibilities that we hastily agreed to a contract well before we ever stepped foot in the building.

When we were finally able to go inside, we discovered extensive water damage beneath the structure that would have made repair costs extensive (not to mention expensive). Now, I would never recommend putting a contract on a property before actually seeing the inside, but it was a church for heaven's sake, with a nursery and pulpit, and all the fixin's. Being a fan of taking risks had led me to excitedly work towards my dream before all the details were worked out. Although, as with People's Chicken, in the end, I had to pull the plug on the purchase when it came time to write a check. Still, our team's mind had already been transformed. Our dream had evolved into a bigger vision: that creating this space was about much more than simply having a facility for Chick-fil-A leadership meetings. I was no longer looking for a meeting room, but a place where we could invest in the next generation.

This new frame of mind led us to discover nearly fifteen acres of farmland near our restaurants. The land, which included an old house, creeks, fencing, and a barn, was going to be developed into a residential community. The property had a rich history: Not only had the same family owned the land for 100 years, but they also allowed the community to create incredible memories during that time. Its visitors had uncovered countless arrowheads in the creeks from when the Cherokee roamed the land centuries before—and this history was something we wanted to preserve. I felt like a steward of this land. Although it had been a family horse and cattle farm for a lifetime, trees and weeds had taken over the property, and the facilities had grown dilapidated. Since the property had not been maintained for many years, it needed a lot of love. Completing the project would be no pleasure cruise in the South Pacific, to be sure— but our dream was to transform it into a spot for community connection; a farm where relationships could grow. Where others saw an abandoned, 106-year-old house with slanted floors, we saw so much more.

I was determined to take the first step, to share our vision with our friends in the community and see where it would take us. So, on a big wall in the house, we wrote down twelve of our greatest dreams for our new space. It would be a place where you could host a wedding or a bluegrass concert, where team members could grow a garden. We even threw in the lofty dream of opening our third Chick-fil-A franchise there for good measure. And, just like that, the FARM was born.

Our overwhelming joy was suddenly tempered when just days after the purchase, there was a tragic car accident that killed four students from the University of Georgia. One of the girls who died, Christina Semeria, had attended our church's youth group. She had been a spark in the dark; a very special person who lived with passion, serving guests at Chick-fil-A and working with youth at Young Life. She had embraced life in the form of the music and blog posts she created, writing about a God who loves us and about her hope to be a light in the world.

At her funeral, I found myself sitting next to a man named Kevin Gantz, whom I'd met the year before when he spoke about his goal to relaunch the Young Life ministry at a nearby high school. After talking at length about our cherished community, Christina's legacy of hope she shined, and the steps Kevin had made in his ministry, I told him about the new FARM and our dreams for it. Slowly but surely, we got around to the possibility that Young Life might be able to use the FARM to grow their dream as well. As luck would have it, a run-down house and two dreams were all we needed to get going.

Kevin and I reached out to our community of friends to share our vision and folks rallied with us around the new creation—even though we had *no concrete plans* in place. We were *freestyling* (because sometimes that's how dreams work best!) when my friend Ben Looper at Southeast Restoration joined in. He donated his time and expertise to uncover what was buried behind years of growth with bulldozers. His crew headed up the demolition efforts and began taking steps to see what God was unfolding in the restoration of that house. Then other folks joined in and helped convert the dilapidated barn into a pavilion with a stage.

Isn't it amazing how God surprises and delights us when we simply look at our dreams as the first step on our journey of discovery? Within three years we had achieved *all twelve* of the dreams we'd painted on the wall inside the house. We created a Kindness Trail that covers more than a mile around the property, complete with bridges, benches, swings, and signs that encourage people to reflect on the land's history, the steps they're taking, and the legacy they want to leave behind.

And still, we keep dreaming. Someday the FARM will be a resource for families and youth going through life's tough situations; a counseling center for parents fostering and adopting children; a center for families who are battling cancer and need love; a space to provide hope for families in the throes of overcoming addiction; a creative place to engage the next generation of dreamers, and so much more—all surrounded by donkeys and miniature cows. Though the FARM has a robust future that's still being written, it wouldn't be what it is without the people who pursued their vision for it. And aren't you glad they did? Aren't you glad there are people like Christina, Ben, Kevin G., and you?

You and your dreams are fuel for the next generation. The young people I'm working with today are the kinds of people who dream bigger than this life, and there is so much power within them, especially when they feel unleashed to go after big dreams. One day my friend Jonathan, a college student and leader at one of our restaurants at the time, texted me a photo of an iceberg. Although only the tip of the iceberg showed above water, below the surface sat a huge block of ice that was ten times the size of the tip.

Alongside the photo, Jonathan wrote, "163 cars moved through the drive-thru this morning between 9 and 10 a.m." It may not mean much to you, but it was possibly the fastest-moving hour at a drive-thru in the history of mankind; it is the Daytona 500 of fast-food drive-thrus. But that wasn't how Jonathan saw it. You see, he followed his first sentence with another, more powerful one: "Just the tip of the iceberg." Here he was, moving a record number of cars through our line, and Jonathan had the foresight to imagine that we were *just getting started*. That belief led the number of cars to surpass more than two hundred in an hour during breakfast, and we keep climbing. He proved then that he knew something I am still learning every day: there's much more waiting to be discovered beneath the surface if you just dream bigger.

And no dream is too big! Think of Nelson Mandela, who fought against Apartheid and withstood being imprisoned to lead the nation of South Africa toward a better future. Think of Malala Yousafzai, who became an advocate for female education in Pakistan, and around the world, after being shot by the Taliban. Think of Prince Harry, who left the royal palace to serve his country in the British Army Air Corps. Think of Ellen DeGeneres, who faced discrimination with bravery to inspire millions. Think of Oprah Winfrey, who changed the very fabric of the entertainment industry despite having been born to a teenage mother in poverty. Aren't you glad there are people like Jonathan, Nelson, Malala, Harry, Ellen, and Oprah? I sure am!

There are many who came before me, who didn't know me, but who fought for my freedom anyway. To not pursue our dreams with the same grit is to dishonor the triumphs of their work. I seek to be full of love, knowing that I must fight the ways of this world. Those ways will always try to suck us in. With our focus constantly split between our families, friends, households, and businesses, it is so easy to get distracted. A simple habit that has always kicked my mind toward things that matter is setting aside a percentage of my income to give away to charity. This is not a preacher asking you to give but a businessperson knowing the fun of investing your resources. There is no greater investment than what we pour into others. And it takes daily grit to move the needle on holding firm to the work that matters. Don't just put worms on hooks but put the pole in the water and get to the actual fishing—get to doing things that matter!

If ever you think your dreams won't come true, consider this: years after I set out to meet John Mellencamp, my family and I went to Hilton Head, South Carolina for summer vacation when we overheard a lifeguard mention that John Mellencamp had been playing football on *the same, exact beach* earlier in the day. The next afternoon, my brother and I headed straight for the spot where the lifeguard said John had been playing. And what do you know? There he was, playing football! After freaking out as you might expect, I looked up. I took a deep breath, summoned some courage, walked up to him, and said five small words: "John, can we join in?" As soon as he *irrationally* said yes, I quickly appointed myself to his team and sent my brother to the opposing side. It took a lot of years and a little luck, but my dream of meeting John Mellencamp finally came true—and it was better than I ever dared to imagine.

You just never know where your road trip will take you over the course of your life. If your dream is big enough, odds are the drive to your dream will suffer some detours. You might spin your wheels looking in the wrong places or knock on a few doors no one will answer. Your journey may take hundreds of course corrections. The shots you take throughout the adventure may not play out the way you thought they would. The timetable for your dream may require a decade or two before it becomes fully alive. It may not happen in this lifetime and that is just the beauty of a grand dream. But wouldn't you rather come close? Wouldn't you rather be glad you tried?

It helps to remember that optimism is the key. Consider the win inevitable and go for it, just like we did when we wrote down our dreams for the farm. Think of your success as bold determination with a risk of failure. Just start in that direction. Who knows? You could end up in a football huddle with your guitar hero throwing you a long one down the sandy beach.

KINDNESS PAUSE

What is your favorite thing that somebody created?
Which John Mellencamp song is your favorite?

CHAPTER 12

A NEW DAY

"If you can't fly then run, if you can't run then walk,
if you can't walk then crawl, but whatever you do you
have to keep moving forward."
- Martin Luther King Jr.

I didn't start my career at Chick-fil-A thinking I would someday operate three restaurants. It was never even an option to consider because, at the time, Truett Cathy founded his unique business model with such a focus on local ownership that he hoped each franchisee would operate just one location. Furthermore, franchisees were not supposed to own another business or work another job so that they could pour everything into their one restaurant.

Years later, as restaurants were increasingly built in closer proximity to each other, the policy evolved. The change meant an existing franchisee could be granted permission to operate a second location. Chick-fil-A continued to grow. Around 2015, our headquarters announced that, in rare circumstances, a franchisee could be granted a *third* restaurant. However, Chick-fil-A's operator selection is based on many factors and for that reason, franchisees are not guaranteed to be chosen simply based on the proximity to other locations.

It was against this backdrop that our team got excited when Chick-fil-A, Inc. announced that a new location would be built in our Canton community. We dreamed of being selected as the franchisee for that location, and so we began a years-long journey filled with emotional highs and lows. Through it all, I clung to one consistent theme: the topic of joy. Standing in front of our team at the beginning, I expressed the idea that our joy could not be dependent on whether we were selected. I reminded them and myself that our brains can play tricks on us when we want something really badly; it can convince us that only getting the thing we want will bring us joy. We have to get our minds ahead of this kind of thinking and remind ourselves that joy can be found in what we already have today—in time spent with friends and family; in service in the community; in hope for a better tomorrow; and in loving others, here and now. After all, we may not be given tomorrow. So, while it's fun to explore big dreams and work toward them, reaching the end of each goal should not be what determines our happiness and joy. As long as our basic needs—food, shelter, and safety—are being met, everything else is gravy—And I *love* gravy.

As a team, we had to constantly remind ourselves out loud that our value and joy was not dependent on getting a third Chick-fil-A restaurant. The final determination about whether Chick-fil-A would grant us another location was something over which we had very little control. At one point, we were told that I wasn't even eligible to be considered. That was our reminder that God does not guarantee us anything, except today. If today is all we have, what are we doing to appreciate this day? What kind of dad am I being? What kind of friend? What am I doing with the joy that is available right now? Because our joy is there, wherever we are. It's as close as the people we work with, love, and serve. When you remind yourself where joy comes from, it removes stress over the small stuff and lets you focus on being your best each day. The spirit of joy would be the one thing I needed —more than I ever expected —during our two-year journey.

When we made it to the final stretch of the selection process, our key leaders were getting ready to present their case to some of the top executives at Chick-fil-A. The execs were all set to visit our restaurants for at least four hours to see if we had the capacity to handle another location. And our plan was to end the experience with a speech from Gwen, my wife who was going to come in as "the closer" and share how impactful this opportunity could be in our community.

Because Gwen had previously scheduled a routine appointment with her doctor for earlier in the day, she agreed to join us as soon as it was over. Then I received a text from her that said the doctor was doing some tests and she would be late. She further explained that her doctors had some concerns and were running biopsies. She finished her appointment and arrived at the restaurant just in time to say hello as our visitors were leaving. We had given the review process our best effort over the course of two years and the outcome was now out of our hands.

The next day, we received the call that I will never forget from Gwen's doctor. She explained to us that Gwen had two forms of breast cancer and asked us to come into the office, immediately. Recognizing that her mother had died from the same disease four years earlier, Gwen's diagnosis hit us like a ton of bricks. Life is like that. Your path can take a hard right out of nowhere and quickly sharpen your perspective about what's truly important. Gwen's diagnosis wasn't easy news to adjust to; in no way did it seem simple or kind. As our incredible business opportunity crashed into the hard realities of life, we were forced to face the irrational idea of discovering joy right where we were.

As the days unfolded and our new journey began, our family started the search for a strategy. We sought to find clarity amid tremendous grief and fear. Being in a position that made us feel so scared and vulnerable also made it feel like the healing process would be long and hard. Being that this was not a path we could clear on our own, we formed a team. At times, we all need other people on our team to help forge our path forward. It doesn't take much; if you have one other person in your group, then you have a team; if you can find two people, then you have a community. So, we found the people we wanted to form our medical team, people we could trust and walk alongside, one step at a time.

Several weeks later, we received another call I'll never forget: We had officially been selected for the new Chick-fil-A franchise, which was scheduled to open in sixty days. Once again, the realities of life butted up against our business opportunity. While we were extremely excited, we were equally grounded by our previous mindset—the one that meant our joy would not be defined by a single decision. In response to the unexpected curveballs, we took a page from Gwen's book and practiced redirecting our minds toward the hope found in each new day. Then, more than ever, the parallel worlds that contained our excitement and our fears needed to rest firmly on the irrational thinking that we could find joy by believing in better days ahead.

While I had known that life was hard, that it could deal some major blows and incredible struggles—like illness, death, and loss—it was during this journey that I truly learned to embrace the fact that I didn't, and couldn't, know everything. I learned that when stinky days stink, we must shower them with transparency, honesty, and authenticity. I learned to look inward and admit that I don't want to be a poser or a know-it-all who minimizes other peoples' thoughts, problems, and challenges. The world doesn't need people who claim to know it all, are quick to judge or make things black or white, but it needs people who are willing to admit that most things come in varying shades of grey.

I'm not suggesting that you shouldn't stand up for the things you believe in. What I am suggesting is that you can't know everything because you didn't create the world. Neither did I, and what seems clear to me may not be so cut-and-dry to others. I'm suggesting that we can all stand to get off our high horse, sit down, be quiet, and listen because it can be difficult to view the world through different lenses (plus, I'm scared of high horses anyway). We can believe things to be fact before turning the page and realizing we read the situation wrong. It seems we can make this mistake often in life. I have learned that often we think one thing is a fact when, in fact, we *don't* always have all the facts.

Maybe you're reading this now and thinking to yourself, "He just doesn't get it. He doesn't understand my situation." And you might be right. You see, I am learning more and more each day that it's easy to live in our own bubbles, furnished with our own perspectives and beliefs, our likes and dislikes. I didn't grow up like you did and you didn't grow up like I did, and that makes our perspectives different. Your skin color, your neighborhood, your parents, your financial situation, your failures, and your successes all contribute to the way you view challenges, other people, and the entire world. Just because you think you know what someone else is going through or how to solve their problem, doesn't mean you're right. You may not be able to see the reality of their situation from your perspective, and we all have to work at seeing what life looks like outside our bubbles.

One thing we do have in common: today. A new day is a dawnin', so let's use it to take a look at the many ways we can approach *today* with irrational kindness. You were created to do more than just exist, and you are loved by a Creator who knows so much more than we do—down to the number of hairs on your head. You only have from now until you're dead to pull this life off. So why not start today? It's a new day, after all. And in every new day, there is a new chance to make new discoveries and find new perspectives.

I often think about life as if it were broken up into different percentages: 80 percent of the hours we're awake are filled with the busyness of things like work, school, and relationships, while the other 20 percent is open for us to create new perspectives and angles. Can you paint a new picture of yourself in this 20 percent? One where you're intentionally sowing seeds of growth, gratitude, and joy that will prepare and propel you toward whatever is down the road?

One day, I found myself driving a van full of high school students in the heat of a North Carolina summer. They had given up a week of their vacation to volunteer and they were tasked with replacing old flooring, painting, and repairing the decks of homes that belonged to people who needed help. It was good they were there because I am the worst handyman in the world! If you ask me to fix something that I need to use tools for, it's like asking me to solve an algebraic equation of a linear derivative. Playing to my strengths, I served instead as a great chauffeur and gofer boy.

As we piled back into the van at the end of a sweltering workday, I called out, "Who wants to go get some ice cream?" Amid the deafening cheers, I realized that we only had a short amount of time to make it back to base camp, so any stops for ice cream would have to be fast. I quickly looked up the closest ice-cream shop on my phone and found one about 20 minutes away. After seeing the word "Creamery," I clicked on one of the search results, opened the address in Google maps, and started the race to secure some Cookies-and-Cream. As we drove, it became clear that my decision would make us late, but I figured snagging some of North Carolina's finest ice-cream would be worth the risk.

We screeched into the creamery parking lot and noticed there wasn't any signage anywhere. Strange, for sure, but we brushed it off and kept going. One by one, the teenagers piled out of the van and rushed to the door. Only upon entering did we notice what I had missed in my hurry to find ice-cream: this was a *crematorium.* Yes, this youth leader had taken all these students to a place that burns dead bodies—not somewhere that churns cold cream. Mistaking a crematorium for a creamery doesn't just make for bad ice-cream; it's just plain wrong. Ultimately, our rocky road to secure a sundae or scoop of gelato was made so much sweeter, filled with a great story and plenty of laughter. Plus, it's always fun when you leave a crematorium alive.

You may be taking intentional steps toward the ice-cream shop of your life and accidentally wind up somewhere else entirely. You may find that the least expected trips are where you find the most joy on your journey. Gwen sure taught me that during her bout with cancer. In the year that followed the opening of our third location, Gwen set the standard for taking one day at a time. At the start of every new day, she continued to look up, put hope over fear, and seek joy even during the most difficult circumstances. I'm happy to report that today she's cancer-free and that is a gift we celebrate daily.

What steps are you taking to embrace the joy in today? For

starters, if you need restoration, go take a nap. If you need to break out of self-isolation, go find a hand to hold or a person to serve. If you demand perfectionism from yourself or others, go find some humility by building a wall of failures. See how margins, service, and imperfections can lead you to embrace new irrational perspectives. Let each step toward irrational kindness highlight the fact that we are not here to *just survive.* We are here to *experience the joy* of the journey—a journey on which you are never alone. This is the beautiful news you can share with the world to prove that light overcomes darkness. Make the decision today to choose grace over fear and watch as the light of hope breaks through. Even at times, when life takes you to a place far from where you intended to go, embrace the joy found in the kindness and laughter your new vantage offers. Look up and know I love you—so does a big God in heaven. Also know that as long as you have a new day, you're just getting started.

KINDNESS PAUSE

How do you personally kickstart a positive day?

CHAPTER 13

PERSISTENCE

"When the whole world is silent,
even one voice becomes powerful."
- Malala Yousafzai

I have a memory from long ago that's still so vivid in my mind that it seems like it was only yesterday. You know the kind. I was sitting in the back seat of my Papa's car when my grandmother told me we were going to steer a cow. I had no idea what that meant. Since I was spending a few days at their farm, I would have found out soon enough, but I couldn't wait another second. When I asked for details, my grandmother replied that my Papa and I would take a male cow and make it a steer. I pressed further, inquiring about *how* exactly we were going to do that, and the words she spoke next still ring in my mind to this day. She creatively explained, "You cut its flapjacks off."

I imagine you may be thinking the same things I thought that day. "That can't possibly be a thing, can it?" "Have they lost their minds?" "Are they in some sort of satanic cow cult?" The next day, all my questions were answered. With the calf's mother beating down the door next to us, my grandad and I painted purple medicine all over the patient's private parts and performed surgery with just a razor blade and a needle. Sure enough, we cut his flapjacks off. Without ever intending to, I took part in a life-changing event—life-changing for me, for sure, and certainly for the cow too.

Some things happen in life that are simply life changing. We may not intend to take part in them and in most cases, we can't stop those things from taking place. We can't control everything that happens to us. (Be thankful we're not cows!) The good news is, with persistence and determination, we *can* change many of the things that happen next.

Years ago, the former U.S. President Calvin Coolidge said persistence beats education, talent, and great intellect. That's great news for folks like me who are in short supply of education, talent, and great intellect because persistence starts with just showing up. More than how much knowledge you know, take pride in how much effort you show. Employers will pay a hefty sum to have someone who simply shows up on time and stays until the job is done, so if you develop reliability as a certified signature move, you're already halfway to success.

The best way to practice persistence is simply to strive toward being the best version of yourself. Don't practice persistence in trying to be something you're not. For example, I'm not a synchronized swimmer. Sure, I can hold my breath for an epically long time underwater. Seriously, I've won every who-can-hold-their-breath-the-longest competition my family has ever had, but my body does not flow like a porpoise. Heck, I don't even like getting into pools that much. And while we need time to practice persistence none of us has an infinite supply of time. Therefore, we need to be picky about where we choose to invest our time.

Focus your persistence specifically on exploring areas in which you *want* to grow. If I don't want to be a synchronized swimmer, I don't need to spend my time practicing elaborate dance moves or wearing fancy bathing caps and nose clips underwater. Instead, I can concentrate on treading water in the vicinity of greatness, investing my time examining where I am today and where I want to be tomorrow. That way, I can figure out which steps I need to take to close the gap and become the best me I can be. Keeping an eye on the steps that lead toward continuous improvement can simplify your options and clarify the decisions right in front of you—even when it isn't easy to understand *where* this improvement is going to take you.

I specifically remember when the late Apple CEO Steve Jobs announced at the Macworld conference that Apple had invented a new cellular phone. It was January 9, 2007. By then, Apple had already turned the music industry on its head by making digital, portable songs available on its iPod mobile digital device, so entering the mobile phone space seemed like a natural next step for them. But for me? I was still perplexed by why anyone would think it necessary to bring a phone and a camera together. For years they had been two separate things and joining them together never seemed like a problem that needed to be solved to me. It may be difficult to imagine today, but at the time I could *not* get my head around the advantages of combining them. But, boy, have I learned my lesson since then. The lesson is this: if we keep striving for continuous improvement, it may just take us to a spectacular future we can't even get our heads around, yet.

Apple understood persistence. They didn't wait until they had figured out *every* feature that would ever be on the iPhone before they rolled it out. They just shared the first *version* with the public for starters. And while we were enjoying our new iPhones, they were hard at work creating the second-generation iPhone. Understanding that strategy makes it easy to imagine that behind the scenes they were also probably in a nearly constant state of vision casting for the next iPhone versions 3, 4, and 5, and so on; each time knowing that not all of their ideas would come to fruition. Still, Apple stayed focused on whatever versions were to come down the pipeline sometimes years before they would be released. Corrections, additions, bad ideas, successes, and failures were all part of each version's story.

If, for instance, you were the human version of the iPhone 3, what features would you want to see in the iPhone 4? What does the next version of you look like? What about versions 6 and 7—years down the road? Brainstorm ideas. Write down features you can't even understand how to build yet. It doesn't matter where you're from but where you're going. Heck, you don't even have to see that far. I have some of the worst eyesight of any seeing person in the world—my glasses look like coke bottles, and because of my nearsightedness, without them I'd have to sit a book on the tip of my nose to read it—but to begin visualizing the road in my mind, I only need time and imagination.

Being persistent does not mean you have to transition immediately from being the "iPhone 1" to the "iPhone 5," even if you *can* visualize where you want to be. *Patience* is a great friend of persistence. It takes grit—progress not perfection—to learn, understand, and accept that persistence requires patience. Did you get that? Persistence requires patience, which requires grit, which requires persistence. It is an endless world of discovery (and requires courage to do it every day you get up). And when we see folks down the road who are already standing where we want to be, we must remember that the road to get there requires persistence. Pray for the wisdom to understand the next sizable step you need to take to get there.

On every iPhone box, the text reads, "Designed in California." Guess what it says on your packaging? "Designed by God." You are his creation and his design. He developed you from scratch, and he has wired you for growth. All you must do is charge toward continuous improvement.

Don't be afraid of the word *improvement* either. I've been guilty of avoiding the word at times. Admitting that we need improvement could be considered a negative thing; it's like admitting we're not *already* giving our best. But just like I came around to the camera phone, I have learned that *improvement* is actually an amazing word. It's not an admittance that we stink as we are, but rather that we are in a constant state of bettering ourselves.

I imagine this was similar to Katie Ormerod's experience when she became the first woman to land the backside double cork 1080. Don't know what a double cork 1080 is? Trust me, it is hard as a "mother" to pull off. (Don't worry. I make sure I know all the X Games lingo simply by reading my surfer magazines.) Anyway, the backside double cork 1080 is made up of two flips and three rotations on a snowboard, bike, or another contraption that flies. Like I said, hard as a mother. This is probably why Katie started her journey with a twist; she didn't start her journey trying to land this concoction out the gate. Over time, though, she started to add more rotations and her twist turned into a flip. And then her flip turned into a backside double-cork 1080. What Katie did to land the infamous move is the same thing that's required of me and you every single day—we must bravely go after the next version of ourselves, one quarter turn at a time. And as we do, remember nothing can take the place of patience and persistence—with a twist of courage.

Are you familiar with the story of the three servants from the book of Matthew? One day, a rich man gathered three of his workers to look after some of his money while he was away on a long trip. The rich man gave each of the workers different amounts based on the abilities he saw in them. He gave $5,000 to one, $2,000 to another, and $1,000 to the last. When he returned from his trip, he gathered the three men to settle up.

The rich man was immediately pleased because the worker with the largest amount had doubled his $5,000 investment. Likewise, the worker who was responsible for $2,000 had $4,000 to turn in—and the rich man was in awe of him too. The last man stepped up and explained that he only had the $1,000 he'd been given to return. The last worker had been so afraid that he would lose the rich man's money that he simply hid his portion until the rich man returned. While the worker was proud of his play-it-safe mentality, the rich man was not. He thought it was such a terrible waste that he even described it as criminal. Because the rich man was not looking for workers who were just going to get by; he wanted his investments *and* his team to grow. He wanted them to inch ever-closer toward completing a backside double-cork 1080.

In the story, the exasperated rich man took his $1,000 back from the timid worker and gave it to the man who had risked the most with what he'd been given. The master angrily threw the last man out. This reaction could come off as harsh since the third worker didn't technically lose any of the money he'd been given. However, the boss recognized clearly that his worker was more fearful than cautious. He had done nothing to try and improve his circumstances; in the end, he was not judged by how much he had, but by what he had done with what he'd been given. All the master was looking for was a simple step toward improvement. We don't have to make the same investments as others. We simply need to be good stewards of what has been given to us—and invest in becoming the best next version of ourselves.

Stories like this one reshape our minds to approach the world in a fresh, new way. They help push aside old ideas. Just because "this is how it's always been done," doesn't mean that's the only way it should ever be done. Instead, we can learn from the snapshots of Jesus's life that even seem kind of crazy. Let's be wide open to the ideas Jesus laid out that are so irrational, they have the potential to revitalize and reshape the world. Hear his plea to *not* be conformed to the patterns of this world, but rather to be transformed by the renewing of our minds. Let's not allow the seemingly complicated, the harshest critics, and the most expensive needs to freeze us where we stand and limit our possibilities.

Have you ever heard the adage, "Do what you love, and you'll never work a day in your life"? Though I have heard it at many graduations and leadership talks, I've found it to be full of holes. Like I love to sit on the beach, but I have yet to find anyone who would pay me to do so. We work because there's less purpose in life without it. It isn't part of life. It *gives* us life. So, I believe a better version of this quote would be: "Do what you love, and you *get* to work towards something filled with an infinite source of purpose and energy."

Tend daily to the strength it takes to see yourself and the world through a fresh quarter-turn perspective filled with budding hope, vulnerable curiosity, and optimistic thinking. Just as what you eat affects how you feel, and the exercise you get affects the strength of your heart, so it is with your mind. What you pour into it and who you strive to be will affect your positive (or negative) thinking. If you pour the words of negative talkers and junk bulkers into your mind, you let the doubters, haters, and cynics get the best of you. But renew your mind with things not of this world, and fry cooks like us can be wonderfully crazy and positively inspirational in today's landscape.

We have the opportunity to renew our mind by reimagining what is possible. It happens by turning kindness upside down, by giving ourselves and others the margin in which to continuously improve, by shifting our perspectives and approach, by embracing our uniqueness, by failing big yet dreaming bigger, and by finding joy regardless of the outcome. *Kindness* is the challenge laid out in front of us to ourselves and others, and that is by living a completely *irrational* life!

KINDNESS PAUSE

How do I want people to remember me?
What act of kindness can I do for myself that will move me
toward this legacy?

CHAPTER 14

ENCORE

—————

"By the time I was fourteen the nail in my wall would no longer support the weight of the rejection slips impaled upon it. I replaced the nail with a spike and went on writing."
- Stephen King

Years ago, I had the brilliant idea to drop one thousand cows from a helicopter over a park on a Friday night! At only nine inches long, complete with a mini parachute, each stuffed cow would float softly to the ground. The plan was to invite the community to come and catch a cow at a newly opened park. Why would anyone want a stuffed cow that fell from a helicopter? Chick-fil-A—That's why! We painted ten of the cows gold, and promoted the night for weeks, explaining that whoever caught one of these extra-special, golden cows would win free Chick-fil-A *for a year*. When the big day came, we loaded up the cows in huge trash bags and sent Alex and the cows up in the helicopter. Down below, the park filled with eager families ready to catch the coveted cows.

If you asked me, it sounded like a great plan with hardly any room for error. What I couldn't have predicted, however, was how randomly the cows would drop from the helicopter that hovered overhead. Instead of spreading out across the sky like snowflakes, they came down in bunches at different times and in different areas of the park. "Pandemonium in the park" erupted as dads, moms, teenagers, children, babies, and even dogs chased after the skydiving cows. People crisscrossed one another at full speed throughout the park attempting to grab one of the lucky cows from midair. Attendees abandoned strollers and blankets everywhere; kids got lost and children cried amid the clamor. You would have thought it was raining money!

In the end, police had to lock the park down until all the children were accounted for—which they were. Thankfully, as I had hoped and prayed, no one was seriously hurt, and everyone left with their own families. Though the cow drop turned out not to be as foolproof as I thought, certainly, no one could say it wasn't an adventure.

The same stands true for this book. I am by no means a know-it-all, but I'm not a know-nothing-at-all either. I can't know how my plan to encourage irrational kindness will unfold, but my hope is that these pages will continue to lead you to an inspiring new adventure. Some days you'll find great joy in the journey; and some days it will all go to plan; and some days, like the day of my infamous cow drop, things will go unexpectedly sideways.

Any great adventure has the potential for hiccups. In fact, I even saw this theory play out while writing these words! For me writing this book felt like trying to create the next great Van Gogh painting. It was a challenge. I ran into many roadblocks. I wanted to quit. I also wondered: *Will it be worth it? Is it even any good? Is my voice even needed? How do I find the time to finish?* Doubt such as this can be a difficult place to live.

Like me, you may be crafting your grandest dream only to see it get swallowed up by the urgency of ants in your pants, as I call it. That's where the most urgent issues are biting you at the same time, and you must immediately get those ants out! Sometimes life just happens. We can't let these types of urgencies drown out the important work of keeping our dreams alive. Therefore, we must keep grinding: finding the right color to add, the right brush to use, and the right place to paint. With continuous improvement, a little failure, a lot of help, and unrelenting endurance, one day you'll look at your masterpiece and realize just how far you've come. In that way, living an irrational life is a lot like making your own art; it comes together little by little, one version at a time.

Remember, at the beginning of the book, when I told you I wrote a song called *Check Your Gauge*? Well, I recently re-recorded it with the help of some talented friends. And the song, which was originally written over thirty years ago and strummed to life with just three chords, was resurrected in a fresh and exhilarating way. I put the new version on iTunes and invited everyone, anywhere in the world, to listen to it. If you're in Kathmandu and you want to hear it, no problem—I got you covered! Now, I didn't see that coming when I first started playing guitar. I couldn't have dreamed that would even be remotely possible thirty years ago. At the time, the technology didn't exist. I didn't have a single friend with a studio. I didn't even have the musical skill to understand how the song might sound with more instruments. We can't always see far enough down the road to know where we'll end up, but we can get pretty dang far as long as we check our gauge along the way.

The best part? Your story—your song, your art, your life—is

still being written. And as you add to or re-record the song of your life, you can courageously start fresh each new day. So, make it a song you like, and make it beautiful. Learn from other people who are there to accompany you and get better. Stand side-by-side with those around you when you face obstacles and mistakes. Support one another until you find harmony again. Then get up tomorrow and do it all over because the whole world and its future generations are begging to hear your song. I want to hear it, and so does Jesus.

With every step, he is on the sidelines cheering you on, shouting "Yes!" At every stumble, he is encouraging you to feel the rumble from the chant: "I can do *all things* through Christ who strengthens me." And no matter how many promises he has made; they are all followed by a resounding yes and amen. Your song isn't only on his iTunes playlist—it's on repeat!

Now, it is true that uncertainty in this world can burn out even the most optimistic person and tempt that person to give up. But pull that chin up to look up and hear the voices that are cheering you on, see the options, and realize a big world. Seeing a new view that every day is a chance to record an updated version of your masterpiece; little by little, journaling your journey or mapping your route, to figure out where you want to maneuver next.

Simply by caring for this earth and the people in it, we become stewards. And, yes, that includes caring for yourself! Armed with that hope and understanding, I encourage you to become stewards of irrational kindness. First by taking the time to reframe your mind each day, as you hold up your chin to see the love story all around you; and then as you plant yourself firmly on a foundation of promise and hope for tomorrow. Let the love and promise guide you as you go after your pursuits, and let it encourage you to be kind to those around you.

No matter who you are or what you're working on, be men and women of courage; trusting that you're not alone as you put kindness over everything. Whatever is playing during your day, hit pause for kindness. Give kindness its own margin. Consider the wise words of my friend Bob Goff, who asks, "It may be working for you, but is it also working for those around you?"

The only way to know for sure is to be open, honest, and vulnerable about the struggles you're facing—and to invite others to do the same. And don't be afraid to ask for help! If you need a coach, get one. During our own struggles, some of the very best resources my wife Gwen and I have found were therapists, cohorts, and counselors. Surround yourself with all types of people like Jesus did. You don't have to be perfect. However, we should be encouraged to be a little better than we were yesterday.

So, when your cow drop goes sideways or you pick the wrong paint color, know it's not the end of the world. It may simply mean that you get to try a different approach next time. Take comfort in knowing that sometimes the most important things we learn come from the lessons we never expected.

I got one of these lessons from my friend, Kurt Wheeler, who is a songwriter and entertainer by night. During the day, he teaches at an alternative high school, where he educates students who've had challenges at home and in school and who often don't see any hope in tomorrow. Each day in the classroom, Kurt makes sure he tells the kids at least these four things:

1. *You are worthy of an education*
2. *You are worthy of being loved*
3. *You are worthy of forgiveness*
4. *You are worthy of a future*

What does this tell me about Kurt's work in the classroom? It tells me that even if Kurt's students don't remember all his lessons about math, language arts, and science, they know without a doubt that Mr. Wheeler cares about them. They know about the hope he has for them, even if they can't find it for themselves. Kurt gives this kind of hope to everyone he knows, including me. Once, he asked me if I knew how many seeds were in an apple. (There are five in case you didn't know.) And then he said: "We may know how many seeds are in an apple, but we don't know how many apples are in a seed." What makes that promise so great is that *we don't have to know.* All we need to do is keep planting seeds of hope for tomorrow.

It may look like I'm just a waffle fry cook writing a book, but, to me, this book is my apple seed. Not only because everyone who reads it will be presented with the promise of irrational kindness, but also because one hundred percent of the proceeds will go toward supporting families with foster/adoptive children and those in crises around the world. And perhaps this book will be the seed they need to sow hope for tomorrow. Perhaps a waffle fry cook like me can lift the spirits of families who could use a little kindness— the kindness and grace needed to unleash their individual dreams, uncover their unique talents, celebrate their remarkable gifts, and share them all with the world.

If a waffle fry cook can write a book that can do that, then *you* can do *anything*, especially with a little help and kindness between friends. Don't believe me? Come to Canton and see for yourself! Can't come? Write us a letter or send us an email! How ever you reach us, we'll be there, because you always have a friend here in Canton. Heck, you have a whole team of friends here! Our waffle fry cooks want to see you, connect with you, and learn from you, because we know this journey of life is better when we're together.

So, when you can, visit us at the FARM or at one of our restaurants anytime—except on Sunday. We're still closed on Sunday! And let's talk about all our ideas, good and bad, over a cup of medium-roast coffee. I look forward to hearing your stories of growth, love, and forgiveness, thumbing through Surfer Magazine, and hearing about your hopes for the absolutely extraordinary life in front of you—a crazy kind future that you are worthy of!

ACKNOWLEDGEMENTS

Bob Segar sang about the struggle of deadlines and commitments, asking what to leave in and what to leave out. Therefore, I guess I should have known there would be a time I would have to put my pen down. But I resist because I know this story is just getting started— as I learn daily from a growing list of people, on a trek that is still unfolding. This is so different than life or business where you get to keep evolving and creating because this book has an end. I know it doesn't include everything or everybody, and I don't like that. There are thousands who have left their indelible imprints of kindness on my life as they have loved Chick-fil-A guests, team members, community, friends, my family, and me so beautifully. Your wonderful life influence is dispersed throughout these pages.

At the top of my list of people to thank are my parents, Jim and Barbara Williams. My mother's smile and belief in me radiates like bright sunshine all over me. Always cheering and praying for me with arms and fingers crossed regardless if I made the kick or not. My dad's example guides me every step as he walks his talk. They reflected God beautifully by the love they poured into their family and others. Their love for coffee is historic and their availability for a cup anytime to digest the world is a blessing of epic proportions.

To my Tar Heel girl and wife, Gwen, thank you for being my best friend. You not only let me be me, but you inspire me to be so much better. I know God was high fiving, singing, and shouting "Kevin just won the lottery!" with his friends in heaven when you agreed to be my wife.

My children Mary Nell, Terry, Kate and Elizabeth, it is simply ridiculously cool that I get to be your dad. The beauty you bring into the world is why I believe this next generation is going to be the best yet! You teach me how to think from different perspectives and learn from different angles. And, as always, I will have the coffee ready for you in the morning!

Susan Noland and Brad Williams, my older sister and brother, I thank you for forging the jungle of life ahead of me. Your daily wise choices and love for others served as the perfect recipe for me to follow—a recipe of family, fun, and friendship with a little flute and saxophone thrown in. My smile grows as Bart Noland and Susan Williams simply catapult your awesomeness.

Simon and Harriet Dixon's unselfish love for their family is something I am grateful for beyond measure. They cheered for Gwen and I like we were part of Wolfpack Nation at every phase of life.

JK, David, Cooper, Amanda, Carter, Brooks, Henry, Anna Claire, Will, Alyssa, Madeline, Seth, Amelia, Emory, Diana, and Holland...you are my sunshine. I'm gonna watch you shine!

My thinking is inspired daily by the Cathy family as they continue to flip the script on business just like Truett Cathy did. Trudy, Dan and Bubba's brilliant generosity is evident every day. My friends in Generation 3 (Andrew, John and Kylie, Mark, Rachel, Ross, James, and Luke, just to name a few) inspire me today to live out your granddad's life of a good name over great riches. Bring on Gen 4!

I thank my many Chick-fil-A consultants who have influenced our business and my family, including Marshall McCabe, Jay Kimsey, Jim Anderson, Mark Walker, Andy Piper, Blake Sundberg, Jason Ramsey, and Nancy Easterling. I am so grateful for Sonny Newton, Dee Ann Turner, David Turner, David Salyers, Steve Robinson and Jimmy Collins for opening the door for me to step into this adventure by believing in me. I am amazed at my Chick-fil-A friends like Tim Tassopoulos, Mark Miller, Brent Ragsdale, John Bridges, Cliff Robinson, Anita Costello, Andre' Kennebrew, Wayne Hoover, Todd Sweatt, Todd Phinney, Mike Ledford, Jim Maher, Shane Todd, Pat Braski, Doug Barnett, Daniel Trotter, Karen Colley, Cory Wyatt, John Pence, Keith Booth, Scott Hall, Ron Hammock, Andy Duncan, Glenn Jordan, Jonathan Purser, Isaac Holbert, and Brett Lewis along with countless other staff and franchisee friends who give me hope by encouraging and trusting me.

Our Canton, Georgia, Chick-fil-A team is nothing short of amazing in its ability to push me to dream without restraint. Alex Gomez, Cynthia Lara McMillon, Drew Burnett, Jennifer Langston, and Sandy Thompson always make sure not a heartbeat is missed at our restaurants. They operate with an effort of giving their best daily, leading with care for others, and balancing with an incredible spirit of competition. Evident when Cynthia reminds us, "Comparison is the thief of joy...unless you're winning. Then it's totally joyful!"

I owe a huge thanks to Hayden Holcomb, whose creative talent can take an idea and jump in the deep end of the pool with both feet. You believe in our journey and that is why the journey is alive. My insightful and emotionally intelligent mentor Princess

Moon helps me understand the world in new ways. You both are everything to this book.

Thanks to every team member who serves and has served guests at Chick-fil-A Canton, Georgia, and for your spirit of constantly getting better. We can do ridiculous things when we have enough people who care! I use "our" all the time because nothing is about me. It is 100 percent a team effort. Everything is about "team" in fast food, and I love being on your team.

A big thank you to Hannah Brencher, Jenna Johnson, Jenna Carver, Janice Rutledge, Creston Mapes, Krista Morgan, and Annelise Schoups for pushing me to have a point and for encouraging me all the way to the finish line. You ignited my words every time I needed a spark.

Tremendous props to Meghan Brim for your book cover design that is perfection in my eyes! Jess Namynanik for the joy and illustrations you bring to this book and journey. Patrick Dodd for being the most rad encouragers and wisdom givers a friend could ask for.

Literary agents Christy Fletcher and Brian Norman, for wisdom shared along this journey. The entire Morgan James Publishing family, for jumping on board this dream and believing in me is phenomenal. Karen Anderson, Jim Howard, David Hancock, and Gayle West took a waffle fry cook and gave him a chance—thanks for your belief in me.

I am so fired up to have friends like Mark Bradshaw, Chad Teague, Bret Garwood, Joel Parker, Chip Hamilton, Jeff Terry, Brian Thomas, Kirk and Jennifer Saunders, Beth and Scott Sisson, and Michelle and Tommy Holman to name a few—that we get to do life together. Your adventures make life a joy.

To my friend John Mellencamp, who wrote the songs that unleashed my creativity, joy, and songs—and helped me understand my life better. Although I don't personally know you, or if you will ever read this, please know you've had an enormous impact on me from the moment in my driveway I put in *Scarecrow* for the first time. What a day! Seeing one of your paintings in the FARM would be the ultimate! A guy can dream, can't he?

Lastly, thank you Bob Goff for when I first heard you speak, it was like hearing sound for the first time. Your investment in believing and encouraging people is the only reason this book exists. Keep helping us see the world more like Jesus—in totally irrational ways.

LET'S STAY CONNECTED

 Download a free
group discussion
guide on our website

IRRATIONALKINDNESS.COM

 KEVIN@IRRATIONALKINDNESS.COM

 THEIRRATIONALKINDNESSPODCAST

[f] [o] [y]
@IRRATIONALKINDNESS

CHICK-FIL-A RIVERSTONE PKWY
1459 Riverstone Parkway
Canton, GA 30114
770-479-7146
04379@chick-fil-a.com

CHICK-FIL-A CANTON MARKETPLACE
2048 Cumming Hwy
Canton, GA 30115
770-479-0802
02488@chick-fil-a.com

CHICK-FIL-A HICKORY FLAT
6114 Hickory Flat Hwy
Canton, GA 30115
678-493-0091
04120@chick-fil-a.com

THE FARM
4563 Hickory Flat Hwy
Canton, GA 30115

IK!

ABOUT THE AUTHOR

Kevin Williams is one of only a few triple-franchisees within Chick-fil-A, one of America's fastest growing companies. After graduating with a degree in Management Information Systems from the University of Georgia and working in banking, 25 years ago he switched gears to follow his passion as an entrepreneur and restauranteur. He loves walks with his wife Gwen and adventures with his 4 children.

All proceeds from Irrational Kindness will go to the benefit of foster/adopted children & families in crisis.